# DEEP DISCOURSE

BONUS ONLINE VIDEO CONTENT

## A Framework for Cultivating **Student-Led** Discussions

Steve!
Happy reading!
I am looking forward to our partnership.
Sandi Novak
2017

SANDI NOVAK
CARA SLATTERY

Solution Tree | Press

555 North Morton Street
Bloomington, IN 47404
800.733.6786 (toll free) / 812.336.7700
FAX: 812.336.7790

email: info@SolutionTree.com
SolutionTree.com

Visit **go.SolutionTree.com/instruction** to download the free reproducibles in this book.

Printed in the United States of America

20 19 18 17 16 1 2 3 4 5

Library of Congress Control Number: 2016953684

---

# Acknowledgments

We wish to express our gratitude to the many people who saw us through this book; to all those who provided support, talked things over, shared their classrooms through observation and videotaping, offered comments, and assisted in the editing process.

We would like to thank Amy Rubenstein for encouraging us to write this book. We appreciate that she believed in us enough to provide the leadership and knowledge to make this book a reality.

We would like to thank the teachers who opened their classrooms to be videotaped: Kevin Silberman, Pam Schilling, Elizabeth Sletten, Janelle Grueneich, Danielle Christy Sigstad, Lisa Swanson, Aran Hartl, Amanda Lutz, Jennifer McCarthy, and Sharron Stalock. These amazing teachers shined a light for all to see the power of student-led discussions.

And a special thank-you to all the students who allowed us to capture their discussions: it's been wonderful watching them share their talents as both group members and as individuals. By allowing us to listen in on their meaningful discussions, we learn more and become better educators. We hear their cry to let them engage in dialogue with each other more often and we are working to make that happen. We also wish to thank Renee Brandner, Barbara Borer, and Shannon McParland for sharing their leadership and school communities with us.

Thank you to all the educators who read this book and take the journey to expand the opportunities for students to engage in talk with their peers more often. Without the wonderful principals that lead and teachers who model and coach, students' voices would not be heard.

Above all we want to thank our families, who supported and encouraged us in spite of all the time it took us away from them.

Solution Tree Press would like to thank the following reviewers:

Jeanette Brosam
Instructional Coach
English Language Arts I and II Building Leader
Franklin Middle School
Champaign, Illinois

Elaine Dondoyano
Intervention Specialist and Technology Teacher
Rainier View Elementary School
Seattle, Washington

Patrick Kelly
Social Studies Teacher
Blythewood High School
Blythewood, South Carolina

Olivia Lozano
Bilingual Demonstration Teacher
University of California, Los Angeles Lab School
Los Angeles, California

Nicole Mashock
STEM Institute Mentor Teacher
Fond du Lac School District
Fond du Lac, Wisconsin

Heather McDonald
English Language Arts and Instructional Coach
Denver Secondary School
Denver, Iowa

Tryphina Robinson
Assistant Professor of Teacher Education
Shawnee State University
Portsmouth, Ohio

Mary Rodger
Literacy Coach
South Plainfield Public Schools
South Plainfield, New Jersey

Maurna Rome
Grade 3 Teacher
Evergreen Park World Cultures Community School
Brooklyn Center, Minnesota

Jessica Webb
Literacy Coach
Suntree Elementary School
Melbourne, Florida
Williams Elementary School
Rockledge, Florida

Esther Wu
English Teacher
Mountain View High School
Mountain View, California

Visit **go.SolutionTree.com/instruction** to download the free reproducibles in this book.

# Table of Contents

Reproducibles are in italics.

# About the Authors

**Sandi Novak** is an educational consultant and author of *Student-Led Discussions* and *Literacy Unleashed.* She has over thirty years of experience as an assistant superintendent, a principal, a curriculum and professional learning director, and a teacher. Her consulting work focuses on leadership and improving student reading. Since 2010, she has consulted with Scholastic Book Fairs as it partners with schools to improve independent reading. She has worked with schools across the United States to enhance their schoolwide reading cultures. Specifically, she led professional learning and coached leaders to guide professional learning and collaborative practices in their schools.

To learn more about Sandi's work, visit SNovak Educational Services (www.snovak educationalservices.com).

**Cara Slattery** is a teacher leader in the Burnsville-Eagan-Savage School District located just south of Minneapolis, Minnesota. Her passion is teaching learners by sparking their interests and curiosities. She has taught and coached all levels of students from kindergarten through high school. She has led an elementary school in becoming an arts and technology magnet from conception through implementation and sustainability. Cara also coaches teachers to use data in planning instruction, facilitates collaborative teams in reader's workshops, as well as technology and literacy leadership. She has presented at state and national conferences on topics ranging from book talks, technology integration, and student-led discussions and has received the Technology and Information Educational Services (TIES) Exceptional Teacher Award in education.

To learn more about Cara's work, follow @Slatterycl on Twitter.

To book Sandi Novak or Cara Slattery for professional development, contact pd@ SolutionTree.com.

# Introduction

Walk into any U.S. school, enter a classroom, and stay for one hour. Who is doing the majority of the talking? "Typically, teachers ask about 300–400 questions per day and may ask as many as 120 questions per hour" (Vogler, 2008). Who should be doing the talking if we want students to become critical thinkers, problem solvers, and self-directed learners?

The key to having students engage in meaningful dialogue and having groups being more productive is to provide them with explicit instruction, offering guidance along with specific feedback, and then releasing the responsibility to them. In this book, *Deep Discourse: A Framework for Cultivating Student-Led Discussions*, we provide a framework that works in any K–12 classroom. When teachers use this framework, something magical happens: students become more motivated, highly engaged, and knowledgeable about the content.

So, what is a student-led discussion? It's when students generate their own questions, guide the discussion, and facilitate the flow of the dialogue. The teacher's role is to observe, take notes, and provide feedback, while the administrator's role is to ensure these discussions are taking place in every classroom throughout the school and offer the professional learning necessary to promote successful experiences.

The environment necessary for effective student-led discussions cannot be turned on and off throughout the day. In other words, students must feel free to express their thoughts without fear throughout all parts of the day. Successful discussions occur when each student develops his or her own personal insights about a subject, takes on an inquiry approach, contributes to the dialogue, and advances his or her understanding about important topics. Lofty goals, to be sure, but you can accomplish them in a variety of classroom types and sizes.

Student-led discussions are game changers for schools and classrooms. District administrators, literacy leaders, and principals can confidently use this book with teachers at all grade levels. Whether you are an elementary teacher, a reading specialist, a middle school teacher, or a high school instructor, this book is written for those interested in actively engaging students in all aspects of student-led discussions, with a goal of reaching deep discourse. In its professional standards, the National Council of Teachers of Mathematics (NCTM, 2000) describes *discourse* as ways of representing, thinking, talking, agreeing, and disagreeing; the way ideas are exchanged and what the ideas entail. We describe deep discourse as engaging in *high levels of thinking and dialogue* by clarifying, elaborating, building connections, disagreeing, questioning, evaluating, and synthesizing to extend learning and deepen understanding of content. The teachers and examples we use throughout the book represent a fraction of the many who successfully shifted the responsibility for discussion to students. We hope that many more, including you, will attempt to improve on the numbers you'll see in the opening research, allowing students to facilitate dialogue in more classrooms.

In chapter 1, "Articulating the Need for Student-Led Discussions," we introduce the student-led discussion concept as an important instructional practice, share research about using the communication skills in the real world and its impact, and provide examples of teacher-led and student-led discussions.

In chapter 2, "Establishing a Discussion Framework for Student Success," we introduce a framework for successful implementation of student-led discussions in any grade or classroom and describe it with detail and rich examples. After introducing the framework, we embed and call it out in future chapters. We purposefully avoid headings that isolate the framework into discrete steps as it is a fluid process and not a linear progression.

Chapter 3, "Beginning the Journey," suggests ways to get started, provides necessary management tips, and gives a brief look at how one second-grade team begins its own journey.

In chapter 4, "Experimenting With Different Discussion Formats and Strategies," we offer a variety of formats for discussions and share examples using multiple texts, establishing various purposes, and applying higher-order thinking skills.

Chapter 5, "Using Discussion in Different Content Areas," delves into using this framework in subject areas other than language arts by explicitly teaching important skills and strategies that advance students' knowledge in social studies, science, and mathematics.

In chapter 6, "Getting to Deep Discourse," we share how English language arts (ELA) standards can be used as a guide in planning the skills and strategies of discussion, identify how to go deeper, and explain how to embed communication skills while teaching and working on content.

In chapter 7, "Pulling It All Together: Tools and Tips," we summarize the recommendations made throughout the book, offer ways to get started if you are just beginning the journey, and make suggestions to enhance or refine your practices if you are currently using student-led discussions. We provide troubleshooting tips for teachers and then supply administrators with the information and tools necessary to implement and sustain student-led discussions in every classroom throughout the school or district.

Each chapter ends with a reproducible "Take Action!", which prompts teachers to apply their new learning. You can access these reproducibles online and use them as a springboard for professional development work. District leaders also may find them useful in developing a blueprint for implementation.

This book includes companion videos that present views into K–10 classroom discussions taking place in a variety of ways. These videos are referenced in the book's scholar's margins, as illustrated here with video 3.2 "Grades K–10: The Look and Sound of Student-Led Discussions," and show real students engaged in conversation, helping to make the content visible and conveying how teachers, principals, literacy leaders, and district administrators may use the student-led discussion framework in their schools and districts. This video, for example, offers an excellent illustration of the possibilities student-led discussions hold.

At times, the students in our videos appear in small groups with no other students in the background, making some viewers wonder if the conversations are staged. This is not true of any of the discussions, all of which we personally recorded. Often, we pulled small groups of students from the classroom and took them to a quieter space in the school in order for our video equipment to pick up their voices. We offer these videos as a resource to help you on your journey to increase student-led discussions in your classrooms.

We hope this book inspires you, particularly if you are a classroom teacher, to use student-led discussions to empower students as they become strong communicators, collaborators, critical thinkers, problem solvers, and self-directed learners.

chapter 1

# Articulating the Need for Student-Led Discussions

*Student-led discussions motivate me to work with others, inspire me to do more, and change my thinking.*

—MACKENZIE, grade 6

Real-world success requires us to engage with others to learn, create, and produce in hopes of sparking new thinking and learning. Our classrooms are filled with curious, innovative minds that our instructional practices aren't embracing. Our students want to talk—they need to talk!

Although many definitions of discussion exist, we believe one view best reflects the type of discussions we want to advocate in classrooms. Authors Jackie Acree Walsh and Beth Dankert Sattes (2015) define *discussion* as "a process through which individual students give voice to their thoughts in a disciplined manner as they interact with others to make meaning and advance individual and collective understanding" (p. 33). When expectations are clearly set and modeled for students, the students then can take over. The result is meaningful discussion *without* teacher prompting—discussions that promote higher-order thinking skills and use questioning techniques in a meaningful context (Cameron, Murray, Hull, & Cameron, 2012). A certain magic of learning takes over when students become the catalyst for classroom discussions.

## Comparing Student-Led Versus Teacher-Led Discussions

Research supports the value of both teacher-led as well as student-led discussions about text (Hulan, 2010). Although there are critical differences in both formats, conversations deepen understandings beyond basic comprehension (see table 1.1, page 6). Advantages to teacher-led discussions include making a difficult text accessible to students, guiding students into new and challenging themes, and keeping the discussion on topic. A major disadvantage in teacher-led discussions is that teachers "have reduced their presentations to capsules of information and students remain passive consumers" (Byrd, 2008, p. 3). This belief could lead to less thoughtful discussion on the part of students and more reliance on the teacher.

**TABLE 1.1:** Student-Led and Teacher-Led Discussion Comparison

| Student-Led Discussions | Teacher-Led Discussions |
|---|---|
| Students are active participants in their learning and the discussion process. | Students engage in discussions and activities that the teacher designs and facilitates. |
| Students develop their own questions and are responsible for the flow of conversation. | The teacher asks questions, calls on students to respond, and then may ask a follow-up question to redirect or expand on the concept while facilitating the flow of the discussion. |
| Students work collaboratively, often in self-selected groups, with other learners based on need or interest. | Students either work individually or are assigned to work in groups the teacher determines. |
| Learning requires active participation whereby students seek meaning and construct their own knowledge. | Students passively receive the learning, enduring understandings, and set objectives from the teacher through a lecture format and teacher-directed participation. |
| Students monitor their learning with assistance and feedback from the teacher. | Extrinsic motivators like grades and rewards often motivate students to complete work. |
| Students understand expectations and are encouraged to monitor progress through use of self- and small-group assessment. | The teacher primarily evaluates student work. |

Typically, the teacher and teacher-led activities dominate classroom conversations (Kamil et al., 2008; Mercer, 1995; Nystrand, Wu, Gamoran, Zeiser, & Long, 2003). In a study of classroom interaction, Kamil and colleagues (2008) share that "discussion currently accounts for an average of only 1.7 minutes per 60 minutes of classroom instruction" (p. 22). Besides not giving most students time to talk, another disadvantage of teachers guiding discussion is that their questions are primarily closed or procedural (Groenke & Paulus, 2007). Some examples of these types of questions are: Who was the president of the United States in 2000? and How do you solve this math problem? Furthermore, some studies that use Charlotte Danielson's (1996, 2007) framework to collect data for their research find that using questioning and discussion techniques are where most teachers experience difficulty achieving an above-basic rating (Ho & Kane, 2013; Sartain, Stoelinga, & Brown, 2011).

Yet, when students lead their own discussions, their conversations result in higher-level questioning using a whole range of responses, from literal to critical to evaluative. From our observations, when teachers explicitly teach communication skills and group participation protocols there is also wider participation from group members and greater cohesion within the group. Student engagement through discussion can be linked to improved learning outcomes—some of which include higher-level thinking and increased student achievement (Applebee, 2003; Murphy, Wilkinson, Soter, Hennessey, & Alexander, 2009). In this type of discussion, all participants' thoughts, ideas, feelings, and responses contribute to and influence each participant's interpretation of the text. Additionally, conversation has a positive effect on comprehension across all grade levels (National Institute of Child Health and Human Development, 2000).

Good teachers use a combination of teacher-led and student-led discussions to meet student needs. Just like all good instruction, students achieve best when they are exposed to techniques that align with the required learning concepts and instructional demands. This book focuses on student-led discussions because, in most traditional 21st century classrooms, there is an imbalance between teacher-led and student-led discussions. Since students talking with one another can produce great benefits, they warrant additional time, energy, and attention.

## Gaining 21st Century Skills

Learners' access to information is easier than ever before. They can read a variety of texts, watch videos, perform online searches, pose a question for the world on social media, and get answers to most anything in seconds. It is no longer our job as educators to fill their minds with information. Instead, we must teach them *how to learn* in order to ignite their passions, engage their minds, and promote critical thinking and problem solving. Accessing and using information are 21st century skills that are already essential to student learning. More than ever, individuals must be able to perform nonroutine, creative tasks if they are to succeed in jobs.

Although skills like self-direction, creativity, critical thinking, and innovation may not be new to the 21st century, they are vital in an age where the ability to excel at nonroutine work is rewarded and expected as a basic requirement. Whether a high school graduate plans to enter the workforce directly or continue with a postsecondary learning experience, he or she must be able to think critically, solve problems, communicate, collaborate, find good information quickly, and use technology effectively. These survival skills are not only important for career success but also for personal and civic quality of life (Partnership for 21st Century Learning [P21], n.d.).

Competence in speaking and listening is important to students' academic, personal, and professional success. These communication skills help students develop healthy interpersonal relationships, interpret messages, and learn to present themselves in effective and competent ways. It is often assumed that students will learn communication skills on their own, without any formal training. Unfortunately, instruction to enhance students' communication skills rarely exists in schools (Edwards & Edelen, 2009).

Our students no longer depend on the teacher to deliver information, but instead need the teacher to help develop and refine the skills needed when thinking analytically and collaborating with others about content. Teachers guide students to inquire, pose great questions, listen, reflect, respond, and develop conclusions based on new learning. When done successfully, our students gain multiple perspectives on a wide range of topics and are comfortable having deep, challenging conversations with anyone.

Students who experience student-led discussions describe them as being more fun, cool (Cameron et al., 2012), saying they have learned how to talk about a book, found a reason to use the strategies their teachers taught (Certo, Moxley, Reffitt, & Miller, 2010), and many liked reading a book for the first time (Avci & Yuksel, 2011). Students even began swapping books and conducting their own discussion groups outside of class. Students who were typically not interested in reading were begging to borrow books and receive new book recommendations. Isn't this the type of behavior we want from all students?

Think about the last time you learned something new, visited a new place, or read something interesting. Chances are you couldn't wait to share or discuss. When conversations are consistently happening in our classrooms, students are provided an authentic daily audience. Like adults, students love a great conversation about something interesting that stimulates their passion. They love to take a stand on an issue and defend it. They enjoy being excited about something and sharing it with others. They love to read, write about, and wrestle with things that intrigue and inspire them to think differently or have their own ideas challenged. When schools and teachers include these practices that students enjoy, they create environments that put students first, give their voices real audiences, and allow them to take responsibility for the flow and depth of discussion rather than relying on adults to prompt every verbal exchange.

Students need knowledge in core subjects, but they also need to know how to keep learning continually throughout their lives. When students are responsible for carrying out a rich discussion among their peers, they establish an intentional practice of facilitating and participating in collaborative exploration and development, which make up the doing element at the highest levels of learning (Byrd, 2008). Informational learning, in addition to developing skills in communication, critical thinking, problem solving, taking initiative, and working with others, needs to be incorporated into classrooms deliberately, strategically, and broadly (P21, n.d.).

## Fostering Engagement With Collaborative Environments

What does an environment for student-led discussions look and sound like? Imagine walking into a classroom that feels alive and is buzzing with students fully engaged in collaborative learning, discussion, and discovery. It may be a bit noisy at times, students definitely will be out of their seats, and the teacher looks more like a participant than a presenter. Despite appearances, however, students are focused on the same learning goal.

Studies show that students are more likely to be engaged during literature discussion when they have opportunities to (1) respond to one another's interpretations, (2) challenge the author's style, (3) share opinions about text, and (4) question a text's meaning (Almasi, McKeown, & Beck, 1996). These types of opportunities exist within classrooms that foster acceptance of differences, in which students know that their responses are built on, rather than evaluated or dismissed by teachers (McIntyre, Kyle, & Moore, 2006). Teachers who promote collaborative work and sharing ideas create the type of classroom environment where student-led discussions flourish.

## Looking at Instructional Choices

Note the contrast between a teacher-led and a student-led discussion in the following scenario. Pay particular attention to what students are doing in each approach.

Students are invited to suggest a new specialist or alternative class such as music, art, engineering, science, or technology. They are called on to research, discuss, and create a recommendation for their school faculty and administration. This inquiry task requires researching, establishing an argument, gathering evidence, and presenting a proposal to others. Depending on the class structure, the teachers could provide instruction on these tasks through either teacher-led or student-led discussion.

In a *teacher-led discussion*, with which you're certainly familiar, the teacher poses questions to the whole group and calls on students with their hands raised in the air. The called-on students share their ideas and evidence. Additionally, a few students may pose questions or comments in response to others' ideas. This communication pattern, channeled through the teacher, continues for the remainder of the discussion.

You may already see the limitations inherent in this format, but let us dive a bit deeper. Clearly, engagement is at a minimum during this discussion as most students are passively listening, with only a few being called on to share their responses. Although the teacher is very busy managing the classroom, limited thinking occurs and only a few perspectives are shared. Because students sit quietly in their seats and speak only when chosen, it's inherently difficult to determine if students are actively engaged or merely compliant.

Now let's look at a classroom that uses *student-led discussion* as the mode of instruction. First, and you'll learn more about all of this in chapter 2 (page 15), the teacher plans and designs the focus lessons students will need. Next, the teacher selects one or two pieces of text to use when modeling during the focus lessons. These texts relate to a couple of the specialty areas and serve as exemplars of persuasive writing. Students refer to the process the teacher modeled and their practice throughout the course of their independent work, research, or discussion. As the teacher observes groups throughout the inquiry and discussion, he or she may add focus lessons based on student need.

To bring this into clearer focus, consider the following scenario in which the teacher sets the purpose for the discussion, explains the learning targets, and proposes a time line: "The purpose of our discussion is to determine and recommend a new specialist class you believe would be valuable for all students in our school. You will be researching classes that might work well here at Jackson Elementary, and ultimately each group will make a recommendation, with evidence and details to support your recommendation. The learning targets we will focus on during this day-to-day inquiry include: *I can communicate both orally and in writing the elements of persuasion used to establish a persuasive argument. I can use solid textual evidence and provide at least two examples to support my argument during discussion. I can consider and challenge an opposing viewpoint at least once during our discussion.*

"As you know, other learning targets might surface as we begin this work together. I will describe and post the learning targets each day before we begin. What questions might you have before we begin?"

The teacher may involve the students in brainstorming a list, or may give them a list of specialist options that the faculty already selected. Students then select a specialty area of interest, read, and gather evidence from various texts and other media to prepare for the discussion.

In this classroom snapshot, you see all students engaged in different activities, yet working toward the same goal. Students read, take notes, bounce ideas off others, share evidence and examples, and challenge each other during discussions. Ultimately, through their discussion, all students provide input into the proposed specialty area.

As you can see, the teacher is never idle in the student-led classroom. Neither are students. They are engaged, accountable for their learning, and working hard every day. In this classroom, students cannot be passive learners and listeners. They are minds-on, hands-on because their teacher has masterfully crafted their learning by purposefully planning for their engagement. In this environment, students are in charge of their learning, and the teacher supports them throughout the process. Video 1.1 "Grade 4: A Student-Led Discussion Example" exemplifies how several strategies and skills work together during a student discussion to develop ideas, strengthen student thinking, and expand perspectives. In it, fourth-grade students engage in discussion to develop their understanding of a text.

Because achieving this level of student-led discussion is an effort and a time-intensive process, altering the ratio of teacher-to-student talk in this way requires believing in its importance, knowing how to do it, and purposeful planning.

## Moving Toward Effective Student-Led Discussions

After reading about student-led discussions and observing hundreds of discussions in many classrooms, we developed the rubric in figure 1.1 to help you self-assess your practices. School leaders sometimes ask all teachers to self-assess using the rubric to determine professional learning needs within the school.

| Descriptor | Beginning | Developing | Arriving |
|---|---|---|---|
| **Time Allocation** (Grades K–2) | • Students are given opportunities to turn and talk with lots of teacher direction.<br>• Amount of time for students to discuss ranges from two to five minutes. | • Students are given several opportunities to talk in pairs and triads at least daily with assistance from teacher.<br>• Some opportunities go beyond short turn-and-talk conversations.<br>• Amount of time for students to discuss ranges from two to ten minutes. | • Students talk in pairs and triads.<br>• Conversations extend beyond quick turn-and-talk conversation to partner chats, small group, student-led discussions as part of the classroom culture.<br>• Amount of time for students to discuss ranges from two to fifteen minutes. |
| **Time Allocation** (Grades 3–12) | • Each student-led discussion cycle takes about one to three weeks.<br>• One or two student-led discussions occur within the school year.<br>• Amount of time for students to discuss ranges from ten to thirty minutes. | • Discussion cycles take one to three weeks.<br>• Number of discussion cycles increases as teacher and students increase knowledge and confidence.<br>• Amount of time for students to discuss ranges from fifteen to twenty minutes. | • Length of unit of study varies depending on text length and complexity but does not extend beyond three weeks.<br>• Student-led discussions occur multiple times during the year depending on schedule; groups either meet one to two times per week or multiple times during the unit of study.<br>• Amount of time for students to discuss ranges from fifteen to thirty minutes. |
| **Text Selection** | • Whole class reads the same text.<br>• The teacher chooses the text. | • Whole class may read the same anchor text, then teacher provides book talks for students to choose one of three other texts to discuss in groups.<br>• The teacher chooses the text based on books students may like to read. | • Various books are offered based on interest and different readability levels.<br>• Students or teacher may give book talks to introduce texts to class.<br>• Text choices are clustered by similar themes. |
| **Focus Lessons** | • Focus lesson is about how groups should function.<br>• Focus lessons are randomly taught without a planned scope or sequence. | • Focus lessons include mostly content and minimal teaching of communication skills.<br>• Focus lessons include a clear sequence, but scope lacks incremental lessons building on skills. | • Focus lessons include both content and communication skills.<br>• Multiple focus lessons are clustered to teach specific skills growing in complexity, aligned to ELA standards and delivered in consecutive periods. |

continued →

**Figure 1.1:** Rubric for student-led discussions.

| Descriptor | Beginning | Developing | Arriving |
|---|---|---|---|
| **Preparing for Discussion** | • Students read independently or with support.<br>• Teacher provides some questions and the initial prompt to get discussion started.<br>• As students read, they prepare two to three questions for discussion. | • Students read independently or with support.<br>• As students read, they inconsistently apply strategies, take notes, and prepare questions relying on visual cues posted in classroom. | • Students read independently or with support.<br>• As students read, they consistently apply strategies, take notes, and prepare questions without relying on visual cues. |
| **Discussion** | • Students take turns speaking and rely on the teacher's input to guide their next steps.<br>• Students may be assigned roles to better understand the process.<br>• Conversations sometime stall or go off-topic without self-correcting. | • Group discussion flows with an identified student facilitator.<br>• Students assume roles with inconsistent effectiveness.<br>• Conversation flows and strategies are applied with inconsistent results. | • All group members share in responsibility for keeping the discussion going.<br>• Group members change roles based on need.<br>• Conversation flows and strategies are applied with fairly consistent results. |
| **Written Response and Reflection** | • Little or no writing in response to reading or discussion is occurring.<br>• Writing tasks have not been planned when developing the lesson.<br>• Some students are applying rituals and routines for writing tasks. | • Writing in response to reading or discussion occurs sporadically or without purposeful plans.<br>• Writing tasks are randomly planned without clearly aligning to the focus lesson or learning target.<br>• Rituals and routines for the writing tasks are beginning for most students, but they rely on the teacher for prompts and direction. | • Writing in response to reading or discussion happens regularly.<br>• The teacher plans writing tasks and the tasks have a purpose linked to a focus lesson or learning target.<br>• Rituals and routines for the writing tasks are well established and students are able to assume responsibilities with minimal teacher assistance. |
| **Feedback** | • The teacher gives minimal group or individual feedback.<br>• Students have not been taught or they do not use assessment to self-evaluate their individual and group effectiveness. | • Irregular group or individual feedback by the teacher is given and does not link to learning targets or previous feedback.<br>• Students have been taught but do not regularly apply the use of assessment to self-evaluate their individual and group effectiveness. | • Groups and individuals receive regular feedback by the teacher linked to learning targets, previous feedback, or both.<br>• Students have been taught and regularly apply the use of assessment to self-evaluate their individual and group effectiveness. |

*Source: © 2016 by Sandi Novak.*

*Visit* ***go.SolutionTree.com/instruction*** *for a free reproducible version of this figure.*

When using the rubric, you may find yourself in all three categories, noticing strengths as well as areas to learn more about and develop. Student-led discussions change and evolve over time as teachers and students increase their knowledge, confidence, and use within their classrooms. This rubric provides a perspective for this change. Use it to get started or help enhance instructional practices.

As you progress through the book and begin to implement the student-led discussion framework and practices this book describes, revisit figure 1.1 often and use it to guide and gauge your growth in each area.

Chapter 1

# TAKE ACTION!

Use this reproducible to apply your learning and, potentially, as a springboard for professional development work.

1. In the following template, keep track of the opportunities students have to engage in discussions over the course of a week to determine the percentage of teacher-led versus student-led discussions. Invite a trusted colleague or coach to observe and track these data using the provided template. What steps might you take to increase the number of opportunities students have to direct these conversations and engage in rich dialogue about text?

| Date | Teacher Led | Student Led | Topic | Comments |
| --- | --- | --- | --- | --- |
| *2/22* | ✓ | | *Reading comprehension* | *After reading a story, I asked students questions to check their comprehension. I could have students develop questions as they read and discuss in small groups.* |
| | | | | |
| | | | | |
| | | | | |
| | | | | |
| | | | | |

2. Review your lesson plans for the upcoming week and count how many opportunities students will have for discussion and think of ways to increase this number.

3. Use the rubric in figure 1.1 (page 11) to self-assess your status. Which descriptor are you most curious to learn more about?

chapter 2

# Establishing a Discussion Framework for Student Success

*We no longer need to be told what to do and how to do it. We use each other for learning and make decisions about where to go next.*

—CONNOR, grade 7

Consistency and structure are important elements of effective instruction. Implementing a framework for student-led discussions, and using it routinely, builds comfort and confidence with the model. When students know what the structures and routines are, they can move more efficiently through daily procedures. Our students gain stronger understanding of their role in discussion, take charge of their learning, and hold themselves accountable. As this process evolves, we guide students' learning by providing explicit instruction and observing their implementation of strategies and skills while giving feedback to individual students and groups.

## Defining the Student-Led Discussion Framework

Table 2.1 (page 16) breaks down the framework for student-led discussions; the framework can be used in any grade and subject. This framework provides a cyclical model that, when applied consistently, creates discussions that evolve in complexity and rigor. The table lists descriptors of teacher and student actions to guide the process.

The video 2.1 "Grade 2: Student-Led Discussion Framework With Partner Chats" shows what the student-led discussion looks like, with components seamlessly working together, and illuminates the gradual release model for this age group. The gradual release of responsibility (Pearson & Gallagher, 1983) is a model that scaffolds

**TABLE 2.1:** Framework for Student-Led Discussions

| Component | Teacher Descriptor | Student Descriptor |
|---|---|---|
| Focus lesson | Model and provide guided practice in a short ten- to twenty-minute lesson. | Watch, listen, take notes, and participate as guided. |
| Application of learning | Support and reinforce the learning targets. | Apply new learning individually or in groups and move from practicing with teacher support to independence. |
| Observation and record keeping | Observe and record application of learning targets in notes. | Self-monitor their application of learning targets. |
| Feedback | Use notes to provide specific feedback to individual students or groups. | Apply feedback and transfer new learning to their discussions. |
| Reflection | Provide prompts, time, and a vehicle for students to gauge their new learning and guide them to think about their next steps. | Monitor their own progress, understanding of content, and contributions to the discussion through writing, conversation, and thinking. |

*Source: Adapted from Novak, 2014b.*

instruction for students and follows a demonstration or modeling prompt and practice format more commonly referred to as, *I do, we do, you do*. During this instructional delivery model, the teacher explicitly models for the whole group, then has students practice the learning target with partners. Finally, you see the teacher provide feedback to the group about his or her observations as students apply the new strategy. These second-grade students engage in partner chats, in which discussion occur with pairs of students chatting together using the student-led discussion framework.

Taking an extended look at the partner chat process, video 2.2 "Grade 2: Partner Chats" provides an example of pairs or triad groups of second-grade students asking questions and talking about books.

## Focus Lesson

A focus lesson allows students to see and hear their thinking and application of a strategy, skill, or technique. As you apply a strategy to a piece of text, students observe, contribute when appropriate, and possibly take notes to reference later. This explicit instruction gives all students a plethora of skills, strategies, and resources to use before, during, and after their discussion.

The focus lesson is ten to twenty minutes of explicit instruction and guided practice for students. During the focus lesson, we define the *learning target*—the skill we expect students to learn and demonstrate. The strategy is introduced, modeled, and practiced using a text excerpt or picture book. Student-led discussion is not a learning target or a lesson's purpose, but rather a means to achieve an overarching goal to deepen understanding of content. Learning targets address content by linking student talk to reading, writing, listening, and speaking that the teacher explicitly taught through modeling.

It's important to note that each focus lesson you introduce should logically and naturally lead to the next one. Education researchers have long noted the importance of lessons enhancing each other. Jerome Bruner's (1977) approach to curriculum development describes the benefits of revisiting a focus area through a sequence of instruction, with each new level building on prior knowledge and growing in complexity. Therefore, focus lessons should not be taught in isolation. Instead, they should be purposefully planned units of study that use lots of interesting, relevant texts to meet the learning targets (Guthrie, 2001).

In the fifth-grade example we offer later in this chapter, students learn a process of searching for a common theme between texts. By using short examples of text in each focus lesson, you provide several, varied examples of themes developing in different texts. Students can digest in one lesson a short excerpt, consisting of a page; whereas, it might take weeks to read aloud one complete novel, giving us only one text for all focus lessons. This may limit the exposure to various ideas and themes that come with the introduction of many short texts. Furthermore, experts convey that we should consider using short text when we want to *demonstrate* close reading with students (Coleman & Pimentel, 2012; Fisher, Frey, & Lapp, 2012). Students attain deeper discourse when they read closely to interpret the text and use short excerpts before longer, more complex texts are utilized.

It is important that the focus lesson remains short and the learning target focuses on just one piece of content and one communication skill or strategy. Too often we overteach a concept. By the time students are asked to try it, they have lost interest or are confused as to what they are expected to do. One hallmark of a strong and concise focus lesson is the creation of a visual resource, an *anchor chart*, which outlines the critical elements of the skill or strategy being taught. This tool, which the teacher and students create jointly during the focus lesson, is posted in the classroom and is accessible to students to use as a reference during independent and group activities.

Graphic organizers, anchor charts, and sentence stems created during focus lessons are important to display for students' reference. Through research, we know that graphic organizers support student understanding (Dean, Hubbell, Pitler, & Stone, 2012; Marzano, Pickering, & Pollock, 2001; Robinson, 1997) by helping students form mental pictures. Without visual prompts, it is hard for students to move from understanding strategies to applying them during reading and discussion.

When we provide these types of support, we give our students structures that lead to their independence. The more support we offer to students, the faster they are able to move toward independence with rigorous academic tasks. You will notice that they request additional directions or repeated instructions less frequently. Throughout the year, you should revisit and remind students of the strategies illustrated on the charts and sentence strips. Although these supports are crucial to younger students, they are also important for older students when learning new communication skills and strategies to understand and talk about content.

Video 2.3 "Focus Lesson of Main Idea and Supporting Details" illustrates the significance modeling plays during a focus lesson in order for students to achieve the desired

learning outcome, paraphrasing text evidence to pinpoint the main idea. Teachers use modeling to achieve a desired learning outcome.

## Application of Learning

During the focus lesson, you should provide examples and time for guided practice before releasing students to apply their new learning through independent reading and group discussion. With focused instruction and practice, move from a structured, guided activity to a deeper application of learning. You can find examples of this kind of deeper application of learning in chapter 6 (page 105). Now students will use their communication skills to develop deeper meaning and understanding as they discuss the content with their peers.

For students to demonstrate mastery of a learning target, they need to show that they can apply it during guided practice and in their independent and group work time. Transfer of learning happens when they have opportunities to apply their newly acquired skills in novel situations. Although transfer of learning is talked about in educational courses, it rarely happens in classrooms (Fisher & Frey, 2007). When students lead their own discussions, they must choose and apply skills without teacher assistance, making this transfer more likely to occur.

Video 2.4 "Grade 5: Citing Evidence to Support Main Idea" shows fifth-grade students applying their learning by drawing on textual evidence to determine and support the main idea or ideas in nonfiction text.

## Observation and Record Keeping

Effective observation and record keeping are fundamental to good instruction. They enable us to plan, organize, and create a quality learning environment. During student-led discussions, the teacher records data about individual contributions and group performance. The teacher should also make note of class patterns, strengths, and areas for growth.

When planning a lesson, a backwards design approach to student-led discussions helps to identify the look-fors, or indicators, that align with the learning targets. *Look-fors* are the criteria that exemplify mastery of the learning goal. These criteria for success are clearly communicated to students before guided or independent practice, and teachers use them when observing and gathering feedback from individuals and groups. They also provide an excellent self-assessment tool for students. A combination of providing students with opportunities for self-evaluation and goal setting has been shown to improve academic achievement (Schunk, 1998).

Teachers develop their own record-keeping systems to fit their classroom culture, their beliefs about education, and their time constraints. Although the system may be different from classroom to classroom, all teachers should observe and gather anecdotal notes about student interaction with their peers and progress toward grade-level standards. The teacher's role, as an observer, is to provide specific feedback to individual students and groups to deepen their understanding of content and to strengthen their communication skills.

In each grade-level discussion framework example included later in this chapter, you will find a table or figure that demonstrates different styles of record keeping. Each has its own advantages and limitations. You can use them in any grade.

As you select a tool, consider your intended purpose for collecting data and the feedback you want to provide individual students or groups. This may change as your focus lesson and learning targets evolve. Ultimately, select a data-collection tool that fits your work habits and teaching style so you can incorporate it into your daily practice and transfer your observations to future lessons. Make whatever you select doable and effective. Start with one and adjust it until it becomes both natural and useful for you.

## Feedback

Educational consultant and researcher Susan M. Brookhart (2012) informs us that there is more to feedback than just crafting some purposeful, insightful comments. You need to think about what happens before and after you give feedback. Effective feedback directs attention to the intended learning target, points out strengths, offers specific next steps that advance the learning, and allows opportunities for students to use the feedback (Brookhart, 2012; Chappuis, 2012). Video 2.5 "Grades 4–5: Data Collection and Small-Group Feedback" confirms the value of data collection and teacher questioning when giving feedback to students, while video 2.6 "Grades 9, 2, and 5: Feedback" features a variety of approaches to provide feedback.

Asking students to think about their work before receiving feedback aligns with a student-centered environment, where you guide your students into becoming self-directed learners. Peer feedback gives students a voice; their role is vital in one another's learning (Perks & Middleton, 2014). Therefore, one way to begin the feedback cycle, with an individual or a group of students, is to ask, "How do you think you are doing on your learning target today?"

Education researchers John Hattie and Helen Timperley (2007) describe four types of feedback.

1. Feedback about the activity or task
2. Feedback about processing and working on the task
3. Feedback to help students self-regulate in order to monitor and direct their own learning
4. Feedback about the person

These authors describe the first three types as helpful; whereas the fourth is not because it implies that achievement is beyond the student's control. An example of the fourth could be telling a student he or she is smart; that feedback suggests the student is inherently intelligent. The first three types of feedback are applied in the examples found in this chapter.

Students have a greater chance of achieving learning targets when teachers provide ongoing feedback about their progress (Hattie, 2009). Using these data, the teacher shares specific feedback with students and also makes decisions about upcoming focus lessons.

Feedback should improve student learning, have students become more motivated to learn, encourage them to become more self-directed in their learning, and demonstrate that classrooms are places where feedback is valued (Brookhart, 2008). Use students' response to feedback to evaluate its effectiveness. After teachers deliver the specific feedback, they observe its application by students to see if the feedback is moving students forward to the desired next step. We provide deeper examples of constructive feedback in chapter 6 (page 105).

### Reflection

Providing time and structure for reflection is the final, critical piece to the success of student-led discussions. Experience gained through discussion is not enough. Reflection on experience with subsequent action provides opportunities for learning and growth (York-Barr, Sommers, Ghere, & Montie, 2006). This reflection may take many forms—drawing, oral, written. And students may reflect to:

- Advance their learning
- Synthesize content learned during the discussion
- Explore a new or interesting perspective
- Generate questions for ongoing inquiry
- Provide feedback about the learning target or process

In the reflective classroom, you should regularly invite students to make meaning from their experiences.

Oftentimes, the most powerful learning happens when students self-monitor or reflect (Zemelman, Daniels, & Hyde, 1993). Therefore, in order to be most beneficial, teach students to think about what they have accomplished, what they have heard from others, and next steps for their learning. Reflection may occur individually, in groups, after reading, or during student-led discussions; and it may occur at any time during the learning process. Reflection does not have to wait until the end. Use the lesson progressions we provide in chapter 6 as a resource to get you started.

## Putting the Framework Together

Table 2.2 is a fifth-grade example of the framework for implementing student-led discussions (Novak, 2014b). Other grade-level examples are included in this chapter and other chapters throughout the book.

**TABLE 2.2:** Grade 5 Example of Framework for Student-Led Discussions

| Item and Description | Teacher Role | Student Role |
|---|---|---|
| **Focus lesson:**<br>• Teacher models—provides guided practice in a short, ten- to twenty-minute lesson.<br>• Students listen attentively, respond to questions, and get ready to apply learning target. | Teacher says, "Today's learning target is 'I can determine a common theme between two stories and describe four to five specific connecting details to support the common theme in writing through notes and orally within my group.' As I read a short passage from *Fish in a Tree* (Hunt, 2015), I think about details that identify a common theme between this excerpt and the picture book, *Thank You, Mr. Falker* (Polacco, 1998), that we talked about in another focus lesson." | Students listen attentively as the teacher explicitly models the learning target. They apply the learning target through guided practice during short turn-and-talk exercises as part of the focus lesson. (See page 62 for a description of turn-and-talk.) |
| **Application of learning:**<br>• Teacher *supports* and *reinforces* the learning targets.<br>• Students *apply new learning* individually or in groups. | Teacher *supports* and *reinforces* the learning targets as he or she moves among groups listening to their discussions, being careful not to interrupt. | Kaia says, "I think Ally's challenge in the book, *Fish in a Tree*, is like Carley's in *One for the Murphys* (Hunt, 2012) because other kids pick on Ally just like they bully Carley. On page 96 of *Fish in a Tree*, it says, 'And then I think that if someone hung a sign on me that said anything, having that sign there wouldn't make it so. But people have been calling me *slow* forever.'"<br>Felicia says, "I agree Ally believes others think she's stupid, but she doesn't know how to deal with it in the beginning. On page 97 it says, 'I don't know who to be. The one to admit that I can't do it, or the pretender.' So this tells me that she didn't just deal with being dumb right away just like Carley didn't know how to deal with being in foster care at first." |
| **Observation and record keeping:**<br>• Teacher *observes* and *records notes* of applying learning targets.<br>• Students *self-monitor* their application of learning targets. | Teacher notes from observing as a group discusses *Fish in a Tree*:<br>*Marcus understands theme, uses details, supports with evidence about the fish's inability to climb a tree. Marcus doesn't make the connection of this excerpt to the title of the book. Manual links comment to Marcus's point "I agree...," then provides one example of how Ally faces a challenge when she asks Mr. Daniels why she is dumb. Kaia extends the conversation ("I can add to the idea...") by providing further detail of the teacher saying she might be dyslexic—linked to the theme.*<br>**Common pattern:** Students read quotes from book. Next possible instructional step is paraphrasing when citing evidence. | **Students monitor their application of learning targets:** When the discussion gets off topic at one point, Felicia says, "I think we are getting sidetracked. Let's get back to talking about the common theme and details from the story." |

continued →

| Item and Description | Teacher Role | Student Role |
|---|---|---|
| **Feedback:**<br>• Teacher gives *individual* and *group feedback* about strengths, areas of growth.<br>• Students self-assess, listen, ask questions, and apply feedback. | Teacher provides feedback to the *students*.<br>**Group feedback:** The teacher says, "How do you think you did on identifying the theme and supporting it with details from the text?" (*Waits for response.*) "Your group identified a theme—overcoming challenges—in two books you read. You also worked together to support your position with details. Specifically, what details did you talk about that contributed to the development of the theme?" (*Waits for response then provides detailed example of things he noted.*) "When you state examples from the book, sometimes it's powerful to read the quote and sometimes it works well to paraphrase it . . ."<br>**Individual feedback:** The teacher says, "Marcus, you stated a theme and quoted an important excerpt in the book. I noticed that you had a sticky note on that page. Why did you select this excerpt and why was it important?" | Kaia says at one point during the discussion, "I didn't know there could be a number of different themes in a book and that two different books could have similar themes!" |
| **Reflection:**<br>• Teacher and students *reflect on their progress* and their *understanding* of content and determine *next steps*. | Teacher and students together participate in a group reflection.<br>Teacher says, "How do you know that your group achieved today's learning targets? How could you use your new knowledge from this discussion to inform and inspire others to meet challenges they face?"<br>**Next steps:** Teacher says, "During your conversation, I heard evidence that fits with your position about Ally facing her challenges. While I observed, I noticed that you quoted the author directly each time you offered evidence. Another way is to paraphrase what the author said. We'll learn more about that technique next week." | Students provide responses as appropriate to teacher prompts. |

*Source: Adapted from Novak, 2014b.*

When teachers consistently use this framework in their classrooms, students become more knowledgeable about content while practicing and developing their communication and critical-thinking skills. In the following sections, we provide examples for second, fifth, and eighth grades to further explain how student-led discussions are enhanced through the use of this framework.

## Grade 2 Example

In this focus lesson, we break down the student-led discussion framework for a second-grade classroom.

**Reading learning target:** I can find and note two to three similarities and two to three differences while reading two versions of *The Three Little Pigs* story.

**Speaking and listening learning target:** I can present two to three similarities and differences I found, listen attentively as my group members share theirs, and ask or answer questions of the speaker in order to clarify my thinking.

**Focus lesson:** Many focus lessons preceded this culminating lesson. The teacher, Ms. Simmons, does an interactive read-aloud of the text, *Goldilocks and the Three Bears* (Marshall, 1988), noting important details of the story for one of the focus lessons. She models her thinking, records her thoughts on sticky notes, and places them directly in the book. Then, Ms. Simmons writes some of the important details about the story on chart paper to use and reference in subsequent work with students.

In another focus lesson, Ms. Simmons reads *Believe Me, Goldilocks Rocks!* (Loewen, 2012) to her class. While reading, the teacher models her thinking aloud about the similarities and differences between the two versions of the folktale, *Goldilocks and the Three Bears.*

In order to prepare students for a rich discussion, Ms. Simmons models how students can organize all their ideas into a graphic organizer that will help them quickly access similarities and differences about the two versions. Therefore, this topic is featured in another focus lesson in this unit. Also, since students have limited practice with conversing on their own, another focus lesson delves into asking and responding to questions to keep the conversation moving.

Finally, Ms. Simmons is ready for the day's focus lesson, which features noting similarities and differences from two versions of *Goldilocks and the Three Bears* books. Ms. Simmons says, "We have talked about the similarities and differences between two versions of *Goldilocks and the Three Bears*. Strong readers think about how stories are alike and how they are different." She shows the completed anchor chart that they generated together earlier in the week to remind them of the similarities and differences between these two versions of the story (see table 2.3, page 24).

Later, the text selection changes to different versions of the *Three Little Pigs* books, which students then read independently. Upon completion, they talk about the similarities and differences in their small groups. Ms. Simmons tells her students, "During the last few days, you have been reading two different versions of the story about the three little pigs. As you read, you thought about important details, captured your thoughts on sticky notes and placed them right in your books. Each day, you talked with partners and in small groups about the books your group selected to read, noting important details from each text. Yesterday, you organized your thoughts about the similarities and differences by making a chart in your reading-response notebooks similar to the one we have posted here" (refers to the previous example, used in table 2.3, page 24).

**TABLE 2.3:** Differentiating Stories With an Anchor Chart

| Categories | ***Goldilocks and the Three Bears*** by James Marshall (1988) | ***Believe Me, Goldilocks Rocks!*** by Nancy Loewen (2012) | Same or Different |
|---|---|---|---|
| **Characters** | Papa Bear, Mama Bear, Baby Bear, Goldilocks | Papa Bear, Mama Bear, Baby Bear, Goldilocks | Same |
| **Who is telling the story** | Narrator | Baby Bear, called Sam | Different |
| **Why bears left the house** | Porridge was too hot so the bears went for a bike ride | Baby Bear complained about having porridge again so Papa Bear said they should go for a walk until he was hungry | Different |
| **How the bears traveled from home** | Went on bicycle | Walked | Different |
| **What Goldilocks said when tasting the porridge** | Patooie! | Eeeeeww! | Different |
| **Porridge** | • Three bowls<br>• Goldilocks tried all three<br>• Baby Bear's porridge was just right | • Three bowls<br>• Goldilocks tried all three<br>• Baby Bear's porridge was just right | Same |
| **Chairs** | • Three chairs<br>• Goldilocks tried all three<br>• Goldilocks broke Baby Bear's chair | • Three chairs<br>• Goldilocks tried all three<br>• Goldilocks broke Baby Bear's chair | Same |

"You created your own categories and details to fit your books. So now you are ready to have a conversation in your small groups comparing and contrasting these two books. I am going to model how you might talk in your small groups about the similarities and differences. I'll use the two Goldilocks books we talked about as a class. Good conversations use questions to keep them going so we will work on incorporating some questions too. Then, you will get a chance to have a discussion within your small groups using the books you have read."

Next, Ms. Simmons models and writes sentence stems on individual pieces of cardstock for how to start talking about a similarity and a difference, and displays these visual supports for all to use later in their discussions. On one strip of cardstock the teacher writes the sentence stem: "One thing similar between the two stories is that ________________." On another Ms. Simmons writes, "What is another example of ________________?"

Guided practice is a critical component of the focus lesson and takes place after the teacher introduces the new learning. Students will interact with this part of instruction when the teacher informs them that they will think about one similarity or difference from the *Goldilocks and the Three Bears* books and share it with their partners. Then their partners should follow up by asking a question to keep the conversation going. Later, students apply this learning with a similar task when they engage in their discussions using different versions of the folktale, *The Three Little Pigs*.

Teachers often ask, "How do I provide text choice for independent reading that relates to the explicit instruction in the focus lessons of a unit of study?"

For this second-grade unit, two different versions of *The Three Little Pigs* are placed on each table where small groups will work later. Each table has enough copies for each student to read independently. Different versions of the same folktale are available for students' use. Choose two unique versions of the folktale such as *The Three Little Pigs* (Galdone, 1970; Gay, 2004; Marshall, 1989), *The True Story of the Three Little Pigs* (Scieszka, 1989), *The Three Pigs* (Wiesner 2001), *The 3 Little Dassies* (Brett, 2010), *The Three Little Pigs and the Somewhat Bad Wolf* (Teague, 2013), *The Three Little Wolves and the Big Bad Pig* (Trivizas, 1993), *The Three Ninja Pigs* (Schwartz, 2012), *The Three Little Javelinas* (Lowell, 1992), and *The Three Horrid Little Pigs* (Pichon, 2008). After students browsed the two book selections, they chose their small group location based on their interest in the texts.

Although the selected texts for this unit is limited, students are still offered a choice for their independent reading. Access to many books and personal choice drive students to becoming real readers (Allington & Gabriel, 2012; Tatum, 2013; Wilhelm & Smith, 2014). Students' reading volume and understanding increase, and they are likely to continue to read when they have the opportunity to choose what they read (Allington & Gabriel, 2012).

### *Application of Learning*

Using the learning target in the grade 2 focus lesson, students meet in small groups to compare and contrast *The Three Pigs* (Galdone, 1970) and *The True Story of the Three Little Pigs* (Scieszka, 1989). Preceding this small-group work, students have had lots of practice working in pairs and triads. This activity has them working in a small group of four students. They bring their response notebooks with the chart they make, noting three or more similarities and differences of their two texts.

Amirah says, "There are three pigs in both stories."

The conversation flows among group members as they share many similarities and differences between the different versions of the folktale. The conversation moves from concrete examples taken directly from the text to interpretive, analytical thoughts.

Alfredo adds, "The wolf is telling the story in this book (*holds up* The True Story of the Three Little Pigs *book*), and someone that isn't in the book is telling the story in the other book (*points to it*). That makes them different."

Amirah holds up the book *The True Story of the Three Little Pigs* and says, "I know another way they are different. In this book, the wolf doesn't sound or look mean. I think the way he is telling the story makes him sound funny. Look here where it says, 'It seemed like a shame to leave a perfectly good ham dinner lying there in the straw.

So I ate it up. Think of it as a big cheeseburger just lying there.' It doesn't sound so awful that he ate the pig when he says it like that."

Beckett questions, "Do you think the wolf seems mean in the other story?"

Amirah replies, "Yeah! Look at the picture! He's mean!"

Caden quizzes, "Do you really think the wolf in this book (*holds up* The True Story of the Three Little Pigs) had a terrible cold or was he just saying that so we won't think he is a bad wolf?"

Imani responds, "I think it makes the story more interesting. We know about the three pigs but this story (*touches book*) sounds different."

Beckett says, "Yeah. The cops came and the wolf said he was framed so I don't think he had a cold. He was just making up a story so he wouldn't have to go to jail! I thought that was a cool part in this book (*points to* The True Story of the Three Little Pigs)."

The teacher modeled how to compare and contrast using two versions of the Goldilocks book. Then students were able to practice applying the skill using different versions of *The Three Little Pigs*. Different books should be used in the focus lesson (*Goldilocks and the Three Bears*) and the student-led discussion (*The True Story of the Three Little Pigs*) in order for students to read independently and apply the skill without teacher assistance.

### Observation and Record Keeping

Figure 2.1 is a record-keeping chart that notes individual accountability of key look-fors the teacher talked about during the focus lesson. Record keeping allows you to take broad notes about how the group is performing in general. This template, with look-fors, can be adjusted to include items from any focus lesson and is often used when teachers are just starting out with data collection in order to provide general feedback during discussions. The form also allows educators to listen to a number of groups and note patterns across the whole class.

### Feedback

Ms. Simmons asks, "What specific similarities and differences between the two versions of the folktale were shared during your discussion?" (*She waits for responses.*) "While observing your discussion your group talked about many similarities and differences. When you compared the wolves in the two versions of the folktale you supported it with evidence from the text. By citing examples directly from the text, it helps us to better understand the meaning of the story.

"I also want to point out another thing that came up during your discussion. When Amirah talked about the wolf not sounding or looking mean, she had to think about the pictures and the words in the book to make an evaluation or judgment. Her evaluation was that the wolf told the story in a funny way. Next, she went back into the text and read an example of the dead pig looking like a big cheeseburger. Then, after she

| Group: *The Three Little Pigs*<br>Date: *December 15*<br>Group members: *Beckett, Caden, Alfredo, Amirah, Imani* | | | | | | |
|---|---|---|---|---|---|---|
| | Similarities | Differences | Listen attentively | Ask questions | Answer questions | Use book or notes |
| *Alfredo* | ✓ | ✓ | | | | ✓ |
| *Amirah* | ✓ | ✓ | ✓ | | ✓ | ✓ |
| *Beckett* | | | ✓ | ✓ | ✓ | ✓ |
| *Caden* | | | | ✓ | | ✓ |
| *Imani* | ✓ | ✓ | ✓ | | ✓ | ✓ |
| Notes: *Good discussion, all students participated and all students used their books or notes. Students talked about many similarities and differences. Students gave more details about The True Story of the Three Little Pigs. Two questions asked; question required students to understand and evaluate wolf's interpretation of events (he had a cold therefore the story is based on a misunderstanding). Q: Do you really think the wolf had a terrible cold or was he just saying that so we won't think he is a bad wolf?* | | | | | | |

*Visit* ***go.SolutionTree.com/instruction*** *for a free reproducible version of this figure.*

**Figure 2.1:** Grade 2 record-keeping chart.

read that part from the book, she explained to the group what that example meant to her by stating it didn't sound so terrible that the wolf ate the pig by saying it like that.

"When you make an evaluation during your discussion and share your thinking about it, it makes the conversation more interesting and meaningful. It also helps you understand the story more. Can you think of another example during your discussion when someone may have used pictures and their comprehension to make a judgment within this story?"

Caden replies, "Beckett said he thought the wolf was lying about having a cold so he didn't have to go to jail. The wolf looked guilty in the picture he showed us."

"Thank you, Caden, you just showed how we can use the pictures and our own thinking when analyzing a story. You knew that people and sometimes animals in stories make excuses to avoid unpleasant tasks and used what you knew combined with a picture that illustrated it. Great work! Comparing and contrasting *The Three Pigs* and *The True Story of the Three Little Pigs* was your learning target today. It is clear that you found and cited several similarities and differences between the texts."

Feedback that you scaffold will help students self-regulate in order to monitor and control their own learning which will lead to them seeking, accepting, and acting on feedback others give.

### Reflection

During the group reflection, Ms. Simmons says, "I want you to think about ways you each contributed to the group." (*She waits for responses.*) "The questions asked during the discussion brought other group members into the conversation. Then, tell your other group members and me how you supported the discussion by providing a specific example."

The teacher prompts for self-regulation and waits for responses. Beckett says, "I asked about the mean wolf and Amirah showed me a picture."

Amirah then adds, "Yeah, Beckett said that because I read the funny part about leaving a good ham in the straw."

This verbal exchange tells the teacher that the students understand the type of questions and responses they make contributes to their discussions.

## Grade 5 Example

In this focus lesson, we break down the student-led discussion framework for a fifth-grade classroom.

**Reading learning target:** I can determine a common theme between two stories and describe in writing through notes and orally within my group how the author develops that theme by noting four to five specific details.

**Speaking and listening learning target:** I can present my opinion of how an author develops a common theme by (1) using appropriate facts, (2) incorporating relevant and descriptive details, and (3) sequencing my thoughts logically within my group discussion.

**Focus lesson:** This focus lesson is the culminating task of a two-week unit where students read independently, and then determine and talk collaboratively about the common theme between two stories. Group norms, rituals, and routines are well established and functioning without much need for teacher assistance.

During the preceding focus lessons and independent work time, Mr. Zeigler selected texts to assist in the lesson progression leading up to today's focus. Text selections from which students choose for their independent reading are used for focus lessons along with the picture book *Thank You, Mr. Falker* (Polacco, 1998). Offerings for independent reading include the texts *Hold Fast* (Balliett, 2013), *Rain Reign* (Martin, 2014), *One for the Murphys* (Hunt, 2012), *A Handful of Stars* (Lord, 2015), *Fish in a Tree* (Hunt, 2015), and *Life in Motion* (Copeland, 2014). Students each select one book and form groups of four to six students based on their text selection. As a group, students identify their second book from the selected titles.

Mr. Zeigler states, "During yesterday's focus lesson—we reviewed and organized our notes about the theme or themes represented in a couple of texts and described the details to support the themes. Throughout the lesson today, think about the details, characters' actions, or spoken words we have recorded on anchor charts. We used several texts to determine themes. First, we use our read-aloud, *Home of the Brave* (Applegate, 2007), and focus lesson texts from this week—*Thank You, Mr. Falker*, which teaches us about one girl's struggle and triumph of learning to read with help from a compassionate teacher. We also used a passage from *One for the Murphys*, a story about standing up for yourself and accepting individual differences.

"As I read a short passage from *Fish in a Tree*, think about details that lead us to identifying a common theme between the excerpt I read and the picture book, *Thank You, Mr. Falker*, that we used in another focus lesson. When you are in small groups later, you will discuss details from your two books you have read during this unit to determine a common theme between those two texts and support your opinion with details from your books."

Mr. Zeigler then reads the text on pages 80–81 where the author describes Ally's ideas about an object hidden inside a box. Next, he models his thinking about a common theme between this excerpt from *Fish in a Tree* and *Thank You, Mr. Falker*.

"I think a common theme between the excerpt I just read and one from our focus lesson about *Thank You, Mr. Falker* is that both stories have a caring, understanding teacher that brings out the goodness of others," Mr. Ziegler says. "So, I am thinking that the theme could be showing kindness to others. Mr. Falker helps Trisha with her reading just like Mr. Daniels helps Ally overcome her inability to read well. Each teacher has to win the character over with kindness. In this passage, Mr. Daniels tells Ally that of the one hundred or more students he shows the box to she is the only one who has figured out what is inside. Then, he displays his delight in her accomplishment by giving her a high five."

As he models, Mr. Zeigler creates a T-chart like the one in figure 2.2 with the theme they are studying as the chart heading. Each column contains one of the titles.

| **Theme: Teacher shows kindness to others.** | |
|---|---|
| ***Fish in a Tree*** | ***Thank You, Mr. Falker*** |
| Example 1: Mr. Daniels helps Ally overcome her inability to read well.<br>Example 2: Ally understood the box example when no one else did and Mr. Daniels pointed it out to her.<br>Example 3: Mr. Daniels gives Ally a high five. | Example: Mr. Falker helps Trisha with her reading. |

**Figure 2.2:** Comparison chart of two books.

He models writing the details that support the theme from his think-aloud in the corresponding column of the text he is referencing. He offers the following sentence stem for students to use in their discussion and adds it to the anchor chart for later reference.

"I think a common theme between (*text 1*) and (*text 2*) is that they both have (*insert similarities*). In (*text 1*), (*describe evidence using details from text 1 to support the theme*).

In (*text 2*), (*describe evidence using details from text 2 to support the theme*). So, in my judgment the common theme of these two texts is (*insert theme*)."

Rather than the teacher modeling this important component, he shows a short, two-minute video clip of a small-group discussion that effectively uses the sentence stem.

Then, he reads another excerpt from *Life in Motion* and asks students to compare or contrast it to information they remember and is displayed on the excerpt from *One for the Murphys*'s anchor chart. They share their thoughts about developing themes and one supporting piece of evidence with a partner, using the sentence stem posted on the anchor chart. Then, the students hold their small-group discussions where they compare and contrast the two texts they have read independently over the past two weeks.

### Application of Learning

Students have observed their teacher read short passages aloud to the group and model the process of citing evidence from text that contribute to or represent a common theme of two texts. Each student has read two novels from the featured book selection explained in the focus lesson (see p.28). In small groups, students apply the learning target during discussion by sharing details and citing evidence from their books to determine a common theme. The following is one group's discussion as it applies its learning using *Fish in a Tree* and *One for the Murphys*.

Marcus says, "I think the theme of *Fish in a Tree* is that everyone is smart in different ways. When Ally feels dumb because she can't read, her new teacher tells her she's not and then says something really cool on page 159, 'If you judge a fish by its ability to climb a tree, it will live its life believing it's stupid.'"

Manuel responds, "I agree with your idea about the theme, Marcus. Ally faced her challenge of not being able to read by asking Mr. Daniels why she is dumb."

Kaia adds, "I can add to that idea. I agree Ally responds to her challenges because when Mr. Daniels tells her he thinks she has dyslexia and wants her to take some tests, she is scared at first. But she doesn't want to be called *dumb*, *freak*, and *loser* anymore so she listens to her teacher and agrees to take the tests.

"So I think Ally's challenge in the *Fish in a Tree* is like Carley's in *One for the Murphys* because other kids pick on Ally just like they bully Carley. On page 96, it says, 'And then I think that if someone hung a sign on me that said anything, having that sign there wouldn't make it so. But people have been calling me *slow* forever.'"

Felicia says, "I agree that Ally's challenge is that other kids think she's stupid, but she doesn't know how to deal with it when the story begins. Kids tell her that she is dumb, but Mr. Daniels seems to think differently. On page 97, she says, 'I don't know who to be. The one to admit that I can't do it, or the pretender.' So this tells me that she didn't just deal with being dumb right away just like Carley didn't know how to deal with being in foster care at first either."

### *Observation and Record Keeping*

Discussion skills within this group are quite sophisticated; therefore you need to provide more specific feedback to the group as well as individuals in order to continue their development. Figure 2.3 shows a sample record-keeping chart that allows for specific examples. Four look-fors identify the specific feedback that will be provided: (1) identifies common theme, (2) links theme with supporting details, (3) uses notes, and (4) organizes thoughts.

**Group:** *Fish in a Tree*

**Group members:** *(1) Marcus, (2) Manuel, (3) Kaia, (4) Felicia*

**Date:** *March 2*

| Look-for | 1 | 2 | 3 | 4 | Notes |
|---|---|---|---|---|---|
| Identifies common theme | ✓ | ✓ | ✓ | ✓ | *Marcus understands theme, uses details, supports with evidence on p. 159 about the fish's inability to climb a tree; other students contribute to arriving at common theme. Marcus doesn't make the connection of this excerpt to the title of the book.*<br>*Marcus says, "I think the theme of Fish in a Tree is that everyone is smart in different ways. When Ally feels dumb because she can't read, her new teacher tells her she's not and then says something really cool on page 159, 'If you judge a fish by its ability to climb a tree, it will live its life believing it's stupid.'"*<br>*Later, Manuel connects main characters in two stories to determine common theme.* |
| Links theme with supporting details | ✓ | ✓ | ✓ | | *Kaia links comment to Marcus's point "I agree . . ." then provides one example of how Ally faced a challenge when she asks Mr. Daniels why she is dumb. Manuel says, "I agree with your idea about the theme, Marcus. Ally faced her challenge of not being able to read by asking Mr. Daniels why she is dumb."*<br>*Manuel extends the conversation by providing further details that links to the theme.*<br>*Making a connection to the common theme, Kaia says, "I can add to that idea. I agree Ally responds to her challenges because when Mr. Daniels tells her he thinks she has dyslexia and wants her to take some tests, she is scared at first. But she doesn't want to be called dumb, freak, and loser anymore so she listens to her teacher and agrees to take the tests."* |
| Uses notes | ✓ | ✓ | ✓ | ✓ | *Students refer to sticky-noted pages in books or written notes in journals. Know where to find text. Use sticky notes as placeholder for pages in text to quote rather than paraphrase important ideas.* |
| Organizes thoughts | | ✓ | ✓ | ✓ | *Manuel links comment to Marcus's point, "I agree . . ."*<br>*Kaia extends the conversation by stating, "I can add to that idea . . ."*<br>*Teaching point for feedback: Felicia elaborates when she talks about the characters not addressing their challenges in the beginning of the story.* |

**Figure 2.3:** Grade 5 record-keeping chart.

*Visit* ***go.SolutionTree.com/instruction*** *for a free reproducible version of this figure.*

### *Feedback*

In the fifth-grade example, Mr. Zeigler listens in on the *Fish in a Tree* group's conversations. He notes three possible areas that need additional instruction.

1. Most group members quote directly from the text rather than paraphrasing when citing evidence.
2. Marcus does not link the excerpt he quotes about the fish's inability to climb a tree with the book's title, and no one from his group comments on the connection.
3. The text provides patterns for students to analyze, which leads to deeper understanding of character development, yet students do not note these patterns.

To achieve number one, paraphrasing requires the student to think about the text, and then summarize it orally. This process requires deeper understanding than simply quoting an excerpt. Having students paraphrase what they read or heard is a powerful way to check for understanding (Shaw, 2005) and requires explicit instruction and practice. The use of paraphrasing when citing evidence from the text could be the next focus lesson within this unit of study, if the pattern exists among other groups.

Numbers two and three from Mr. Ziegler's notes involve advanced skills that would be best taught in another unit of study or as a minilesson for just this group if other groups aren't as advanced and ready for this work. Just like Mr. Ziegler, we observe, monitor, and take notes during discussions to give students feedback for continued growth and to make teaching decisions.

Using notes and data from the grade 5 application of learning example, the teacher provides feedback to the group that read *Fish in a Tree.* He states, "How do you think you did on identifying the theme and supporting it with details from the text?" (*He waits for students to self-assess.*) "Your group identified a similar theme—overcoming challenges—in two books you read. You also worked together to support your position with details. Specifically, what details did you talk about that contributed to the theme's development?" (*He waits for a response; then shares specific examples from notes.*) "The conversation flowed well by using connecting language like, 'I agree,' and 'I can add to that idea.'"

He goes on to say, "During your conversation, I heard your group use specific and applicable examples from the text. Citing textual evidence triggers thinking, which leads to deeper, richer discussions and enhances your learning. The technique I heard you use when you used evidence to support your claims was to quote the author directly. Paraphrasing is another way to cite evidence and there are a number of ways to use this strategy to enrich your discussion even more than it was today. We'll learn more about paraphrasing evidence in our next unit of study. Good work today, group!"

Speaking directly to Marcus, Mr. Ziegler says "Marcus, you stated the theme and quoted an important excerpt in the book. I noticed that you had a sticky note on that page so you had identified its importance during your reading. Why did you select this excerpt and why was it important?"

### *Reflection*

The following is an example of group reflection conducted at the grade 5 level. Mr. Ziegler asks, "How do you know that your group achieved today's learning targets?" (*Waits*) "How could you work together using details from these texts to inform and inspire your classmates to meet challenges they face in different ways?" (*Waits*) "When Felicia followed Kaia's comment by saying the two characters were bullied, she added that they didn't just face their challenges right away. We call this elaborating on an idea or comment. Elaboration adds richness to a discussion. How did this comment extend your conversation?" (*Students respond.*) "Were there other places in your conversation that someone elaborated on an idea?"

Students may not always be aware of what they are learning and experiencing. During discussion, students may not know how to elaborate on a concept or idea a group member generates. When Felicia elaborates on Kaia's comment about the two characters being bullied, the teacher highlights it during the group reflection time by first telling them why elaborating on an idea or concept is important. Then, Mr. Ziegler defines the term *elaboration*, provides an example from the discussion, and asks them if they could think of other examples of it being used. This example raises students' consciousness about the communication skills they use during their discussion, which may cause them to reflect on their personal skills.

Refer to the videos 2.3, 2.4, and 2.5 "Focus Lesson of Main Idea and Supporting Details," "Grade 5: Citing Evidence to Support Main Idea," and "Grades 4–5: Data Collection and Small-Group Feedback" to provide a visual fifth-grade example of the student-led discussion framework in more detail.

## Grade 8 Example

In this focus lesson, we break down the student-led discussion framework for an eighth-grade classroom.

**Social studies learning target:** I can read and gather five pieces of evidence from a nonfiction article to support my argument for or against slavery.

**Speaking and listening learning target:** I can listen attentively and respond to a group member's position or specific claim, evaluating the soundness of the evidence, identifying when irrelevant evidence is introduced, and following up with an appropriate response or challenge.

**Focus lesson:** Mr. Plucinak shares the learning targets with students and provides explicit instruction for students to understand these goals. He states, "Today, we will learn how we can use information in a nonfiction text to support our position. As I share my thinking about two short articles, I want you to notice how I am capturing important details to support my position.

"News reports told us about the controversy around flying the Confederate battle flag at the state capitol building in South Carolina. We read and talked about the murders of nine African American people in a church there. Many people find it particularly troubling that some state capitol buildings display the Confederate battle flag, a symbol of a regime that the suspected killer is said to have celebrated. Texas officials, for example, ruled that it could be considered too offensive to be allowed on license plates. This ruling was later challenged through the court system, and the U.S. Supreme Court upheld it.

"An opposing view is that many say flying the Confederate flag symbolizes the South's heritage, culture, and military pride and can be displayed without any sense of racism. Does displaying the flag show historic appreciation, or is it a symbol of an era that breeds racism and should not be officially approved? Let me read excerpts of two different views."

Mr. Plucinak projects the opinion piece, "The Confederate Flag Is a Matter of Pride and Heritage, Not Hatred" (Jones, 2015), for all students to see. Students had been assigned to read this text for homework. Next, he shares how he might talk about that author's view in a discussion to support his position for the Confederate battle flag remaining at the capitol building, highlighting excerpts from the text.

Then he projects a second short letter-to-the-editor piece that was assigned for homework, "The Confederate Battle Flag Is a Symbol of Intimidation" (Combs, 2015) and repeats the process using this article to convey a message. After he models how to discuss the different authors' positions, he asks students to turn and talk to a partner about their thoughts about these two opposing views.

Students engage in a brief dialogue and begin to share a few ideas they generated with their partners. This scenario provides guided practice for students and a real-world situation to shape their new learning. Mr. Plucinak can refer to this situation if students experience difficulty when applying the learning target.

Next, Mr. Plucinak introduces a few different articles about slavery. After briefly describing all the articles he selected, he informs his students they may select and read the two to three articles he chose, or search for their own information about slavery. Then, Mr. Plucinak places students in groups of four to five and tells half of the group members to take the position in favor of slavery, while the other members should take the position to abolish it. While reading their articles, students identify key points to support their positions.

### *Application of Learning*

Just as in their guided practice about the Confederate flag during this new reading, students highlight and record information and key points to support their positions. They weave notes from their articles into their discussion. Students come prepared to the student-led discussion with their articles and evidence gathered. They share, build on, and challenge their evidence throughout the discussion. As students within the group elaborate on their positions by reinforcing their arguments with evidence, members listen attentively, take notes as needed, and refute the arguments with countering evidence from text.

Antonio says, "I think that slavery was common and considered 'normal' in 1861 because the vice president of the Confederate States was quoted in the *Savannah Republican* on March 21, 1861, as saying that African Americans were not equal to the white man. He said that white people were the superior race and that slavery was the natural and normal condition for African Americans."

Mohamed adds, "This idea about slavery and how African Americans were treated led to the crisis that threw the United States into a civil war. How can subordination of any group be good for society?"

Antonio responds, "I disagree with your claim. Not every soldier who went to war would agree that slavery and the status of African Americans were the reasons for their fight. Many Confederate soldiers did not fight to keep slavery and many Union soldiers did not fight to end slavery. President Lincoln even claimed that the Civil War wasn't about slavery or civil rights but to preserve the Union."

Anisah says, "White settlers benefited from slave trade and labor; and slavery was important to the development of North America. Without slaves, few would have prospered and we wouldn't be what we are today. In this article, it says that white southerners argued slave labor contributed greatly to the nation's wealth. The Constitution counted each slave as three-fifths of a person in the census for the purposes of representation in congress and the Electoral College. This gave the South a role in the national government much bigger than its free population would have allowed.

Callie disagrees, "Just because they made money doesn't mean it was right! In this article, it mentions that many white southerners came to believe that growing and selling cotton depended on slave labor. Over time, most took their prosperity for granted. White southerners' wealth was rooted in the work of slaves, and . . ."

Anisah interrupts Callie by saying "Many people from the South feared that without counting slaves as three-fifths of a person, the North could have gained control in congress. Then, the northerners would create taxes on imports, which would ruin the South. The economy would have crumbled without slaves; we needed them."

Callie says, "Okay, I agree that the South may have needed their expertise and their labor, but we should have paid them! It wasn't right for us to force them to work for nothing. No one is less than . . . Well, all people deserve to be paid fairly for their work and expertise. Even though we no longer have slavery, don't you agree inequities still exist?"

The conversation then shifts to talking about modern-day labor trafficking—a subject discussed earlier in the year. Each student contributes to the discussion mentioning things like how immigrants perform jobs under force, fraud, or coercion; how they are paid below minimum wage; and that employers often use extortion, sexual abuse, psychological manipulation, torture, and violence to trap them into staying.

### *Observation and Record Keeping*

The teacher uses figure 2.4 to record notes during the students' discussion. This record-keeping chart is another way to collect data about specific look-fors and hold individual students accountable.

### *Feedback*

Mr. Plucinak offers the group the following feedback. He says, "Using the rubric to self-assess how you functioned as a group, hold up one, two, three, or four fingers to indicate your group's performance today." He waits for response, and then asks members to explain the rationale for their assessment.

Callie says, "I think we all used our notes and supported our positions with evidence from articles. Anisah's point about the Constitution saying slaves counted as three-fifths of a person in the census and the Electoral College was really good. Other good points were made to support and counter our positions. One thing that didn't work so well was that, in an effort to be heard, I was interrupted a few times before I could finish. But I think this happened because we were all getting totally into the conversation."

Anisah says, "I interrupted you a couple of times because I was excited to share my point. I wanted to share it before someone else said something else and I wouldn't be able to fit it into the discussion. I know I interrupt people a lot. My mom gets really upset when I do this to her."

Antonio adds, "I thought the discussion went back and forth about reasons for and against slavery. I thought it was going to be hard to find reasons to support it, but since it was a common practice back then I found a few things to say to support it. We got a little off the subject when we started to talk about immigration, but overall, we had a good discussion."

Mr. Plucinak questions, "Antonio, you mentioned your group went off-topic. What was said or what happened to take the conversation in a different direction?"

Antonio replies, "Oh, yes. I remember. Someone asked about immigration."

Callie says, "No. I asked if inequities still exist today."

Mr. Plucinak replies, "In order to understand better what you were thinking, Callie, tell me what thoughts you had at that time when you asked the question and the point you intended to make by asking it."

Callie says, "I wanted our group to realize that even though we no longer have slavery, all people are not treated equal even today."

Mr. Plucinak asks Callie, "How did you share your thinking with the group?"

Callie answers, "I didn't because we started to talk about immigration and the inequities that exist now and I didn't get a chance to share it."

| | Antonio | Mohamed | Anisah | Callie |
|---|---|---|---|---|
| **Organization and preparation for discussion:**<br>• Completed reading<br>• Has notes | *Used notes to paraphrase article* | | *Used notes and held up article when she shared evidence* | *Used notes and mentioned article; didn't credit source* |
| **Behaviors during discussion:**<br>• Listens attentively<br>• Responds to group members' claims or positions | | *Asked question, "How can subordination of any group be good for society?"* | • *Responded to Mohamed*<br>• *Supported position that slavery was necessary*<br>• *Cited evidence*<br>• *Paraphrased article*<br>• *Interrupted Callie* | • *Acknowledged Anisah's claim that slaves were needed*<br>• *Asked question about inequities*<br>• *Took discussion off track; didn't come back to link it back to slavery* |
| **Application of learning:**<br>• Shares evidence to support a position<br>• Identifies irrelevant evidence<br>• Challenges irrelevant information when introduced | *Used newspaper article to support claim slavery was common* | | • *Shared white settlers benefited from slavery; necessary for development*<br>• *Counted as three-fifths of a person; linked three-fifths person to interpretation—slaves a role in government greater than its free population* | *Countered argument that slavery was necessary for development with point that they should be paid* |
| **Individual teaching point** | *Contributed to "inequities now" discussion without challenging relevance* | *Supported open-ended questions posed to the group with text evidence* | | *Asked question that took discussion off topic and didn't link back to it* |
| **Group teaching point** | *Conversation didn't come to closure. Teach recording key points during discussion in order to summarize overarching themes or big ideas synthesized following discussion.* | | | |

**Figure 2.4:** Grade 8 record-keeping chart.

*Visit* ***go.SolutionTree.com/instruction*** *for a free reproducible version of this figure.*

Mr. Plucinak goes on to explain that one part of the learning target was to identify when irrelevant information is introduced. "While observing your discussion I noticed that the conversation moved away from slavery because you didn't make the connections to immigration," he says. He provides an example of how it could have been linked to slavery and then records his observation for a future focus lesson for all groups. He also provides specific feedback to this group and observes its application during their next discussion.

Another note Mr. Plucinak made was that the group did not bring the discussion to a close. Since this same observation was made in all other groups, he uses this information in planning the next day's focus lesson. At that time, he features the skill of summarizing the key points into an effective conclusion, followed by guided practice and small-group application. This additional work also allows groups to polish their skills of engaging in a discussion where they need to defend a position with supporting evidence.

### *Reflection*

Following discussion, Mr. Plucinak asks students to independently complete a written reflection using the following prompts. In doing so, he wants to know if students have learned the intended learning targets. Written reflection also provides closure and allows students to personally reflect on their learning.

- How is a discussion about opposing viewpoints different from other dialogue you have had about various texts?
- What worked well for your group?
- What areas require additional work to advance your skills or learning?

Student responses will vary because individuals glean new ideas and next steps from their personal learning. Here are a few examples of what students might say.

Mohamed's response to the first question about this type of discussion, "When I was asked to read and talk about articles and information that I didn't agree with, it forced me to take on roles and ideas that I didn't like. I still had to read carefully so I would understand that way of thinking and know what I was talking about during discussion. I had to think ahead about the other viewpoint so that I was ready when challenged by someone else. Discussing this other viewpoint was uncomfortable but it did help me understand the main ideas around slavery. It didn't change my mind, though."

Anisah responds to the second prompt: "Finding evidence in the text and challenging each other during discussion were two areas that went well during our discussion. Everyone was prepared for the discussion which was good. It seemed that everyone had read, understood, and really got into their role—sometimes even getting very emotional. I think we did a good job of challenging each other's comments using the facts like you told us to—and we were respectful like we practiced."

Callie adds, "I want to be more prepared to ask questions during discussion. And they need to be on topic and important so our discussion keeps flowing."

As students reflected on their individual and group work and discussion, what became clear was students deepened their understanding of the feelings, experiences, and actions associated with slavery.

Mr. Plucinak analyzes the written reflections to guide his next steps for individuals and groups. Without this reflection, often our instruction bounces from place to place rather than providing a structured progression of learning for students.

## Applying the Framework

The student-led discussion framework can be applied in any grade and subject. Video 2.7 "Grade 7: Student-Led Discussion Framework in Mathematics" reveals the student-led discussion framework in a seventh-grade mathematics lesson used to analyze student work for errors. Video 2.8 "Grade 9: Focus Lesson and Application of Learning in Social Studies" demonstrates the benefits of explicit instruction paired with student application of learning when watching ninth-grade students engage in real-world, thought-worthy discussions about U.S. gun violence.

Effective teachers create classrooms rich in opportunities for students to construct knowledge, from guided to independent practice. They increase the independent practice's rigor from applying new learning in a structured context to application in novel situations. They offer authentic opportunities that provoke students to confront challenges as they investigate answers to their own questions. They guide and coach students as they hone their skills and dispositions to think and discuss ideas at increasingly deep levels. When students are able to engage in this type of demanding work, they take ownership of their knowledge (Brooks, 2002, 2011). Using this framework helps build students' understanding of content while immersing them in discussions where they apply the skills necessary to function successfully in the 21st century.

Chapter 2

# TAKE ACTION!

Use this reproducible to apply your learning and, potentially, as a springboard for professional development work.

1. Think about an upcoming lesson that requires deep thinking where students might benefit from more discussion about the content. Determine the (1) learning target, (2) content, and (3) speaking and listening skills you want students to apply during their discussions.

| Learning Target | Content | Speaking and Listening Skills |
|---|---|---|
| | | |

2. Use the framework to outline the focus lesson, application of learning, look-fors during observation, feedback, and enduring understandings to consider during refection.

| | |
|---|---|
| **Focus Lesson Description**<br>• Content learning target<br>• Speaking and listening learning target | |
| **Application of Learning**<br>• Group configuration (small group, pairs, triads)<br>• Text used during discussion<br>• Other resources | |
| **Observation and Record Keeping**<br>• Look-fors (one content target and one speaking and listening learning target; one or two other skills that were introduced in the past) | |
| **Feedback**<br>• Will you provide whole-group, small-group, or individual feedback? | |
| **Reflection**<br>• How will students reflect on their learning (journal writing, talk among group through use of prompt, share in whole group)? | |

page 1 of 2

3. Engage students in student-led discussions about a text or topic related to the content you are learning about. While students are participating in discussion, select and take notes using the observation and record-keeping chart you prefer. How will these charts improve the quality of feedback students receive?

chapter 3

# Beginning the Journey

*Starting was the hardest part, but now I help others in my class with reading more because we get to talk to our friends about it.*

—GABE, grade 3

In order for anything to thrive and be successful in the classroom, the teacher and all students need to be invested, engaged, and active participants in their learning community. Student-led discussions are no different. They call on us to establish, create, and maintain a classroom environment where all students contribute equally, are cared for, and respected. Roles need clear definition and students must hold themselves and others accountable to the established and practiced expectations. The teacher must think, plan, and instruct differently in order to create a content-rich environment that ignites students' minds and passions through discussion.

## Establishing Momentum

When we are apprehensive about beginning something new in the classroom, it is usually because we fear it won't go well. We don't know enough or we aren't sure if our students will achieve to our expectations. We already know the content, we're getting to know our students more each day, and we are hungry for students to use their energy in positive ways for learning. These ingredients are the recipe for a successful start.

We should begin with confidence, knowing that every learner will become a stronger reader, writer, and communicator through consistent discussion. Too often our most needy students are pulled out of these discussions because teachers believe the task is too difficult, the text is too hard, the student doesn't talk and is too shy, or writing is a struggle. The truth is, we pull students from these discussions to read isolated passages, answer lower-level questions, rarely respond in written format, and only use teacher prompts for discussion.

In classrooms with high numbers of students living in poverty, teachers talk more and students talk less (Lingard, Hayes, & Mills, 2003). We also know that English learners in many classrooms are asked easier questions or no questions and rarely have to talk in the classroom (Ho, 2005). Let's think about a student who struggles. Wouldn't it seem logical and absolutely critical for this student to engage in student-led discussions as much as possible in order to become more fluent and stronger in reading, writing, speaking, and listening?

## Creating a Positive Learning Environment

Like anything else in the classroom, strong classroom management and relationships are central to success and are equally important for student-led discussions. If we want students to care about different opinions, feel free to express themselves, help and challenge each other, and feel safe, then we must take time to establish solid relationships among all students and adults in the classroom. "Creating an environment conducive for student talk is critical in ensuring that students really do talk" (Fisher, Frey, & Rothenberg, 2008, p. 71).

Establishing a classroom environment with respect and trust is a necessary first step in building a culture where students engage in meaningful discussions. Our students know when their voices matter and they are heard. It is then that they are able to confidently communicate and collaborate with their peers through discussions about text, video, or other media.

How does a teacher begin to establish an effective environment where students talk more and become self-directed learners? There is a strong link between academic success and social-emotional skills (Elias, 2006). Building a community among the learners in a classroom increases student engagement, elevates the depth and rigor of student learning, and establishes an environment where students feel comfortable taking academic risks. Morning meetings, conversations, activities, play, storytelling, games, writing, and collaborative problem solving are a few different ways we can help students build trust and respect for their peers at any level. These simple activities for building trust are essential steps for deep discourse to occur later.

Elementary teachers might begin each day with all students engaged in a morning meeting that includes four components: (1) greeting, (2) sharing, (3) group activity, and (4) news and announcements. The morning meeting is a component of Northeast Foundation for Children's (2007) responsive classroom approach, which focuses on creating and maintaining a community of learners. The *responsive classroom approach* is designed to create classroom environments that are more community oriented, productive, and academically engaging, thus emphasizing both social and academic learning.

Morning meetings give students a positive start to the day, allow students to get to know each other through sharing, and ground students in the academic focus for the day. Whether you use this approach, or something less formal, the practice of developing relationships and trust is essential. Often, teachers are concerned about the amount of time seized from core learning to what they might consider *fluff* or nonessential activities. This consistent investment, however, creates an environment where students feel free to interact, trust one another, and engage more deeply in learning. In everyday terms, we refer to this strategy as *starting slow to go fast*.

Although our secondary school class periods are often shorter than those in elementary classrooms, and we often assume students are beyond such activities, don't be fooled. All students crave a sense of belonging and want to know their presence and input matter. Student-led discussions and deep discourse at the secondary level require a strong, cohesive learning community. In a secondary environment, it is critical to help students forge new partnerships and groups for discussion beyond already formed friendships. Opening activities that encourage talk and facilitate multiple interactions put students at ease and prime the pump for student learning and discussion.

Teachers who are apprehensive to invest critical instructional time on relationship building can incorporate these interactions while at the same time building background knowledge or teaching content. For example, in a social studies classroom, you could take the activity *two truths and a lie* to the next level by telling students to craft their truths and lie about a historical figure, event, or concept. Regardless of the task, all teachers should spend some time providing students with ongoing opportunities to get to know each other and interact through less rigorous activities before expecting them to work productively in groups.

## Setting Expectations for Discussions

Student-led discussions are most successful when consistent structures are in place and the teacher articulates and models clear expectations for discussions. Following this modeling, guided and independent student practice give the teacher opportunities to provide feedback to students while moving from group to group. Allowing students to help create expectations increases their buy-in and successful use in the classroom. Once you develop expectations, post them somewhere in the room where they are accessible for students to practice. Figure 3.1 is an example of one fourth-grade classroom's expectations.

| Before Discussions | During Discussions | After Discussions |
|---|---|---|
| • Be prepared.<br>• Have an open mind throughout the process.<br>• Take notes about things you may want to contribute.<br>• Be sure to think about the new strategy and how to apply it. | • Participate.<br>• Take turns speaking.<br>• Speak clearly and with good volume.<br>• Listen attentively.<br>• Invite others into the conversation.<br>• Challenge others respectfully.<br>• Respond thoughtfully.<br>• Support your ideas with evidence.<br>• Apply the new strategy taught by the teacher. | • Write one personal goal to improve your skills for the next discussion.<br>• Reflect and write some thoughts about the discussion in your notebook.<br>• Jot down important information you learned. |

**Figure 3.1:** Grade 4 discussion expectations.

When designing instruction and preparing for student-led discussions, it is critical that you don't assume students already know how to do what you are asking. You must explicitly teach students how to communicate, be effective group members, transition between tasks, handle and care for classroom materials and supplies, and follow other procedures that assist in creating a positive environment for rich discussions to take place.

In the beginning, creating roles that align with the expectations help students to become proficient in one targeted area, encompassing one expectation. Students change roles and master additional expectations. Roles may include *facilitator, summarizer* or *synthesizer, researcher, presenter.* To learn more about defining and setting up roles for students you may want to check out Harvey Daniels's work with literature circles (Daniels, 2002). Once students have learned and practiced the various roles, they no longer need to be assigned. Roles eventually become unnecessary, as student discussions have a natural ebb and flow and students take on many roles during discussion.

Learning together in groups is most effective when students clearly understand the teacher's goals, are expected and taught to explain things to one another instead of just providing answers, and when group activities supplement rather than supplant teacher-led instruction.

When teachers create and enforce expectations entirely on their own, they limit the amount and depth of learning that can take place in the classroom. By properly releasing the responsibility to students, learning in groups has positive social and cognitive benefits for students of all abilities (Bowen, 2000; Gillies, 2008; House, 2005; Johnson & Johnson, 1985; Law, 2008; Meloth, 1991; Slavin, 1987; Surowiecki, 2004; Walsh & Sattes, 2015).

This gradual release of responsibility model (Pearson & Gallagher, 1983) is key to facilitating student independence and has often been explained as, *I do* (teacher modeling), *we do* (guided practice), and *you do* (independent work). The basic premise is that students learn new skills and strategies through explicit teaching and modeling, receive guided practice with support to apply the new learning, and then move to independent application.

## Creating Learning Targets

We want students to engage in deep academic oral discourse using rich content vocabulary and grade-level language, rather than just talk; therefore, it is incumbent on you to teach them how and provide many opportunities for them to practice. After you have done some informal work establishing a trusting culture, you can begin the more structured process of student-led discussions by providing focus lessons on key topics, strategies, or skills to use when students talk about text, videos, or other media.

As described in chapter 2 (page 15), a focus lesson is a short lesson to demonstrate strategies, skills, or techniques that students will apply in their own discussions. Teachers introduce the strategy, skill, or technique; model it; guide student practice;

offer other examples; and talk about how to apply the strategy, skill, or technique during their reading or within their discussions.

During the focus lesson, the teacher informs students of the learning target. Learning targets convey to students the destination for the lesson—what to learn, how deeply to learn it, and exactly how to demonstrate their new learning (Moss & Brookhart, 2012). Learning targets differ from goals in that they are written in student-friendly language, developed to be shared, and understood by the learner who is responsible for applying them.

Teachers just beginning the process with their students often select only one learning target for the focus lesson. After successful completion of a few focus lessons, they identify two learning targets to develop both content understanding and communication proficiency. When using two higher-level learning targets, students may need multiple opportunities to work toward proficiency rather than just a single exposure. Figure 3.2 lists examples of how content learning targets (language arts and science) and a communication (speaking and listening) learning target can complement each other during discussions. They feature different grade levels for the sake of variety.

In video 3.1 "Grades 4–5: Content and Speaking and Listening Learning Targets," a fourth- and fifth-grades combination classroom teacher explicitly teaches the learning target through modeling and guided practice. The content learning target for the lesson is *I can change my thinking as I read and think about the text*, while the speaking, listening, and writing learning target is *I can jot down how my thinking changes as I read and think about the text and later share these changes within my book club discussion.*

| Grade | Language Arts Learning Target | Speaking and Listening Learning Target |
|---|---|---|
| 4 | I can compare and contrast similar themes or patterns of events in stories through writing. | I can share reasons and provide evidence to support the comparisons I make about themes or events in a story with my discussion group. |
| 7 | I can explain in my written notes how the story's theme develops over the course of the text. | I can listen attentively to a speaker as he or she explains how the story's theme develops over the course of the text and ask a question to encourage the speaker to elaborate. |
| | **Science Learning Target** | **Speaking and Listening Learning Target** |
| 3 | I can combine two or more substances and list the properties that are different from those of the original materials. | I can differentiate between the two substances. I put together and explain the properties in the new substances that are different from those of the original materials. |
| 9 | I can compare and contrast my findings from the experiment, in writing, with those presented in a text, noting when my findings support or contradict the explanation in the text. | I can listen, evaluate, and respond thoughtfully to a speaker's reasoning and use of evidence when he or she presents his or her findings and compares them to the text. |

**Figure 3.2:** Content and communication learning targets.

## Selecting a Text

Many teachers introduce student-led discussions using one book or a short nonfiction text with the whole class. By using one text, you can teach the process of student-led discussions and some strategies for identifying passages for students to talk about later.

After becoming familiar with the process, you can inspire students to read independently and in high volume by providing a variety of texts. You still might use a single text with all students when modeling during a focus lesson in class; however just one text is rarely suitable for *all* students. A sixth-grade classroom might have students reading at a range from second through ninth grades. This range provokes the need to teach students strategies for comprehending all types and levels of text during reading.

Reading one text as a whole group, and discussing it over a period of several weeks, does not support movement up the staircase of increasingly challenging texts called for in the Common Core or any other ELA standards or curriculum. To apply their learning in new and novel ways, students search for and select multiple texts and articles for their independent reading. They need frequent and consistent opportunities to read widely in order to develop automaticity, fluency, vocabulary, and knowledge about content.

## Using Classroom Time

Class periods in K–12 classrooms may range anywhere from thirty to ninety minutes, making time management of instruction and student activities an important component during the planning process. Allotting students time each class period to apply the learning targets from the focus lesson or lessons is critical and requires adhering to a consistent lesson structure with a focus lesson, student activity or discussion, and closure.

In a thirty-minute class period, a focus lesson should take anywhere from five to ten minutes. Teachers can use the remaining twenty to twenty-five minutes for students to independently read articles, books, view media, write, or create a product about the topic. It is often difficult for teachers to imagine this type of instruction happening in just thirty minutes.

Let's take a peek at a lesson that does just that. The teacher delivers a five- to seven-minute focus lesson with the following learning target for students: *I can share a sentence, word, and an image to* summarize *and* synthesize a key point *or idea that supports my argument.* The teacher rereads a portion of text with a focus on making his or her thinking visible for students. While reading, the teacher highlights a couple of quotes from the text that support his or her argument and then records his or her brainstorm about each in the margins. In this scenario, students have previously learned and practiced writing summaries.

This day's lesson encourages students to refine their summaries and synthesize information in the way the teacher models. During the last part of the focus lesson, the teacher posts one sentence, one word, and one image to Google Classroom (https://classroom.google.com) that summarize and synthesize the key point she is making. Using Google Classroom to post answers gives students the capability to read and respond to other students' responses, either during the class period if time permits, or at a later time in school or at home. The entire focus lesson is multimodal, presented aloud and visually. For the application of learning, the teacher invites students to use the next fifteen to twenty minutes to do the same thing with their own text. She circulates and assists students or provides feedback as needed during this time. The last two minutes of class are spent revisiting the learning target as a whole group and asking students to self-assess their understanding by writing their responses in their reading journals.

The next day, the focus lesson specifies explicit instruction through modeling, or with video, on communicating the summaries and synthesis. Independent reading in the previous day's lesson is replaced with student-led discussions.

You need to be mindful when transferring this example to a longer class period. For instance, a fifty-minute class period doesn't mean you will use the whole period to talk. Instead, monitor and adjust time as necessary to align with your intended learning targets and student objectives for that day. A fifty-minute class period that mirrors the two thirty-minute lessons in the preceding example would include a ten-to-fifteen-minute focus lesson, followed by thirty-five to forty minutes for student activities or discussion. Some days require more instruction, while others include less teaching and more student-led collaboration or discussion. Student-led discussions could take place during the student activity minutes a couple times a week or more often, during a smaller chunk of time.

Determining a specific learning target and refining the delivery of a focus lesson with guided practice expands the amount of time students have for activities and discussions. The content, information, and skills attained and strengthened during student-led discussions are far more valuable to a student's understanding than listening to the teacher lecture for too long.

## Making Use of Reading Time

Independent reading is a critical factor in discussions. While students are reading independently, the teacher is busy conferring with students, listening, and providing feedback to a small-group discussion, or reteaching a specific skill or strategy to an individual or a small group. Students are choosing various texts, applying the strategies and skills learned during their focus lessons, and preparing for the next discussion.

If you want students in your classroom to immerse themselves in text for learning, you first must teach them how. The Common Core heightened the importance of providing students with the opportunity to practice by regularly engaging with complex literary and informational texts and to use evidence from these texts to support learning. Students actively read, write, and discuss these texts to build background knowledge and develop a comprehensive knowledge of core content (National Governors Association for Best Practices [NGA] & Council of Chief State School Officers [CCSSO], 2010b).

Intermediate teacher Donalyn Miller (2009, 2013), author of *The Book Whisperer* and *Reading in the Wild*, expects her students to read in volume from a variety of genres each year. This reading volume is necessary to create strategic readers who love to read, know how to apply knowledge from text, and master the skills with proficiency called for in the Common Core State Standards (CCSS) or other state-based ELA standards. Professors and researchers Irene Fountas and Gay Su Pinnell (1996) inform us that students in intermediate grades and beyond should read 50 to 75 books in a school year and students in primary grades that read picture books rather than chapter books should read 100 to 125. According to author, professor, and researcher Richard Allington (2006), a potent relationship exists between the volume of reading and reading achievement.

Primary grades students are learning the foundational skills to become lifelong readers. They focus on learning how to read, strategies for selecting just-right texts, and building reading stamina. Conversation as an instructional tool is well researched, yet it is not used often with reading in the early grades (Almasi, O'Flahavan, & Arya, 2001; Berry & Englert, 2005; Christoph & Nystrand, 2001). Even though students in primary grades may be engaged in only one or two student-led small-group discussions during the year, they should be talking and responding verbally to text regularly. Primary-grade teachers report this work is best done with students sharing with partners first. Once students experience success with their partners, they can work in triad groups.

Often, we rely on skills to be taught throughout the first years of a student's educational career and place less importance on learning to read beyond this point. The CCSS address this old belief that instruction of reading should occur in the early elementary grades *and then students read to learn thereafter.* Most content teachers focus very little, if any, on teaching students strategies to read, analyze, and respond to their content. Yet, all teachers play a critical role in observing and engaging students in reaching deeper levels of reading comprehension—discussing challenging texts assists and builds learners' understanding (Torgesen et al., 2007).

We have an obligation and a responsibility to teach reading and provide time for students to make meaning of the content through discussions in every class throughout their intermediate, middle, and high school years.

All core subjects in school require students to read, analyze, and synthesize key concepts. Depending on the content, however, the text and how well students are able to read and interpret it determine their overall understanding. Think back to a time when students grumbled about reading a chapter in a science textbook that was difficult, or when students had to figure out a complex word problem in mathematics. Rather than tell them to read it again, we must teach students how to read in each content area. All teachers are teachers of reading in their own specialized content area. The skills required to read and analyze a mathematics problem or science article are much different than the skills needed for literature or social studies.

Consider the ninth-grade science teacher whose students are about to begin a study of Newton's laws. The teacher gives students a six-step structure to follow while reading in order to help them elicit key information.

1. Read and study all headings, bold print, captions, photos, tables, graphs, and time lines.
2. List what you know before reading and what questions you have.
3. Read each paragraph or section.
4. After reading each section or paragraph, ask yourself "What does the author want me to know? What is most important? What new questions do I have? Does this make sense?"
5. Note key learning and questions in the margins or a notebook.
6. Partner with another student or meet in small groups to discuss your thinking, questions, notes, wonderings, or key learning.

Providing the time and structure for students to talk to each other results in higher levels of thinking and greater access to content, in contrast with the traditional assigning of a chapter. In this way, students move from passive recipients to active learners through a process that is applicable to any classroom or subject.

## Understanding the Look and Sound of Student-Led Discussions

Successful student-led discussions don't just happen. They are seeded in focus lessons, guided practice, small groups, and collaboration. If you begin with the end in mind, and want student-led discussions in your classroom, you must know what successful discussions look and sound like. Table 3.1 (page 52) highlights some of these features.

Student-led discussions shouldn't look any different than a small group of teachers meeting to discuss an issue or upcoming event. All students sit in a circle at a table, on the floor, or another learning space. Each student is prepared with his or her text, notes, something to write with, and any other needed materials. Students are leaning forward, actively listening to the speakers, offering comments, and posing questions. Often, students take notes, go back into the text, and eagerly await their chance to speak. Students may respectfully disagree, challenge each other, or share different opinions. Strong content is integrated into their discussion. Students are learning together while deepening their understanding, developing their communication skills, and following a structure or process they have learned through focus lessons the teacher shared.

Student-led discussions should sound natural, like a conversation we might have at the family dinner table. At times we get excited, appear passionate, just listen, laugh, or challenge something shared during the discussion. The discussion that ensues,

**TABLE 3.1:** Features of Student-Led Discussions

| Student-Led Discussions Look Like | Student-Led Discussions Sound Like |
| --- | --- |
| • Dialogue about a specific topic with a clear purpose<br>• Prepared with all materials needed<br>• Positive body language<br>• Active listening<br>• Eager to share and respond<br>• Build on one another's ideas with comments and questions<br>• Refer to text for evidence or to clarify and learn more<br>• Active participation in discussion from all members<br>• One facilitator or a role all members share<br>• Teacher observing, listening, and taking notes | • Appropriate conversational volume<br>• Revelations and new learning surface and are evident<br>• Use of lower (factual, closed, direct, recall, and knowledge) and higher (open-ended, interpretive, evaluative, and synthesis) cognitive questions throughout the discussion<br>• Responses build as other members contribute different perspectives, ideas, or both<br>• All voices are heard and respected<br>• Opinions are supported with textual evidence<br>• New insights discovered or questions raised<br>• Use of paraphrasing and summarization skills to demonstrate active listening<br>• Teacher providing feedback to a group, individuals, or both after the discussion |

**VIDEO 3.2**
SolutionTree.com/dd/k10-look-and-sound

following these types of healthy disagreements, results in students re-examining the truths they once had, going back into the text, reflecting, and synthesizing to deepen their understanding. From our observations, we know if students have had a great discussion because they leave energized, continue to discuss the topic or issue with others, and look forward to researching and finding out more to prepare for their next opportunity to talk with others about meaningful content. Video 3.2 "Grades K–10: The Look and Sound of Student-Led Discussions" shows examples of what student-led discussions might look and sound like in K–10 classrooms.

## Letting Go

It is difficult for us to see how learning can occur, standards can be mastered, and problems can be explored and resolved without our constant leadership and know-how in our classrooms. It's time for us to let go and let our students work harder than we do. When we release the responsibility for learning to students, great conversations happen. Consider the following examples of things students have said and then think about the strategies they are using as they communicate.

Jonathan asks, "Jamie, I didn't understand what you said. Can you say it again so I can put a picture in my head?"

Jamie replies, "The video clip we watched about Martin Luther King Jr.'s march from Selma to Montgomery helped me build my background knowledge. If we didn't start with the video and then read the articles, I don't think I would have understood the role the march played in raising awareness of the injustices faced by African American voters in the South and the need for a Voting Rights Act passed later that year."

"Raul, I had a connection when you talked about the characters displaying superhuman traits, and it helped me understand more about the main character," Margarita says.

Raul replies, "I believe that all of these characters were determined. They lived difficult lives and probably were able to survive because of it. Each character showed this trait differently, and all their personal stories were unique. Yet, if I had to use just one word to describe how they are similar, I would choose the word *determined*."

In these examples, students' knowledge of key comprehension vocabulary goes beyond the definitional level and all the way to application in context, which is the goal in all vocabulary instruction.

Consider what students are doing in the classroom when you think about the amount of time spent preparing and designing lessons for students. Are they passively listening? Are they taking notes during a lecture? Are they watching you demonstrate something? Are they applying their learning and deepening their understanding through discussion? Learning is hard work. Students must know that we expect them to perform in ways that match or exceed our expectations as well as their own.

## Teacher's Role

From the start, teachers must design a student-centered learning environment where students have a choice in what they read, are taught strategies for comprehension and communication, and can engage in rich discussion about meaningful content. Next, the teacher must explicitly teach focus lessons with clearly communicated learning targets that students can apply during their discussions. Then, when students begin their dialogue, the teacher has three jobs: (1) observe, (2) take notes, and (3) provide feedback.

It should never be a surprise to students what we are looking for during their discussions. Before they engage in discussion, be sure students know what you are listening for as you listen in to their upcoming discussions. Perhaps you are listening for the types of questions they are using, the textual evidence to support or counter a claim, or the way they describe how characters develop across a text. Whatever it is you are watching and listening for has to be communicated and, ideally, created together with the students.

The teacher listens silently to a group discussion, gathering evidence of student learning, and watches for opportunities to guide student progress by making notes to use when conferring with individuals or group members. A teacher may only meet with two or three students or groups a day to talk about what he or she observed, share strengths, next steps, and what he or she will be watching for next time.

This ongoing, timely feedback is necessary for student growth, yet absent in most classrooms. When students have access to specific, timely feedback, they develop an awareness of their learning, and are more likely to recognize mistakes that help them develop strategies for tackling weak points themselves. Chapter 2 (page 15) includes tools for recording observations, while chapter 6 (page 105) shares several examples of how feedback can be used to extend student learning during a lesson progression.

## Student's Role

In order for an effective discussion to occur, students must come to the group prepared, having read and made notes about the topic or text, developed questions for the group, and, when appropriate, accessed a variety of text about the same topic. At first you might seek out relevant texts for students; however, the ultimate goal is for students to evaluate and self-select text that assists them in their discussions with others.

Students then begin reading and analyzing text—seeking information that will contribute to the group discussion, support their thinking, or challenge once-held perspectives. While reading, it is helpful to provide students with a structure or format for note-taking and gathering textual evidence. With practice, while reading students will independently make notes in the margins of text, write questions, and summarize key information into their response notebooks or similar tools. The response notebook also becomes an important resource for students to use during their discussion. Response notebooks or journals are one tool teachers use often in reading or content areas as a place for students to gather and record their thoughts, impressions, questions, or responses about books, media, class discussions, or any content they have read or learned about. Just like note-taking, you must explicitly teach students how to use a response notebook. Teachers often use response notebooks with students to apply the skills and strategies taught during focus lessons and then encourage students to refer back to these notes and work as needed.

Once discussion ensues, students listen, share, make comments, and ask questions that often lead to new understandings or perspectives they had not considered prior to the discussion. Put simply, we need students to be present during discussions. When students take the lead in determining expectations, we'll find them managing, coaching, and providing feedback to each other. When students own a discussion and are truly leading, all members are contributing to the discussion, referring to their notes or text as needed, and responding to others—they're excited, passionate, and leave wanting more. Video 3.3 "Grade 5: Power of Student-Led Discussions" illustrates the power of student-led discussions as they engage and ignite student passions.

The amount of talk that students do is strongly correlated with their achievement. Effective teachers have lots of conversations occurring throughout the day by actively engaging students in rich discussions to understand content (Fisher et al., 2008). Student-led discussions provide the opportunity for all students to participate in conversations, share their opinions with supporting evidence, and use questions and comments that keep the discussion moving along and going deeper.

## Administrator's Role

Administrators need to encourage student discussions in all classrooms. To that end, they need to know what to look for when they are conducting classroom visits. Later, they will use the information they observe in classrooms as they talk about strengths and guide the planning for additional professional learning.

In chapter 7 (page 137), we provide resources to determine the current status of the students' role in all classrooms throughout the school. We offer a survey that has teachers reflect on their understanding of important elements of student-led discussions. After teachers indicate their level of understanding, they mark how often they use each quality identified in the resource. Principals and district leaders can use this information to determine professional learning needs in a school or district.

We also provide a classroom visit instrument complete with look-for indicators that administrators can use to gather data within a school or district. They can then use the gathered data, in conjunction with the teacher survey data, to analyze and determine a school's or district's strengths and needs relative to student-led discourse and then create a professional development plan based on those findings.

When we explicitly teach students communication and group membership skills in all classrooms, they more quickly and consistently advance their knowledge, understanding, and application beyond what may occur in an individual classroom within a school.

## Grade 2 Example

A team of second-grade teachers has heard about the benefits of student-led discussions and wants to implement them as soon as possible. However, they just can't see how a bunch of squirrelly second graders will manage their time if they are released from whole-group instruction.

After much discussion, the teachers determine that strengthening the reading stamina of their second-grade students will engage them in high-volume reading, provide more time for reading independently, and foster daily practice of the reading skills and strategies taught during focus lessons.

These second-grade teachers begin the year asking students to independently read for five to ten minutes, and gradually increase that amount in five-minute intervals until they can read for thirty to forty minutes. These teachers know if students are able to sustain longer periods of time reading independently, they will be able to meet more often with groups and individuals for guided instruction and student conferences. During independent reading, many students seem to be flying through their books and then become disruptive to those still quietly reading.

After observing students work independently and in small groups, teachers can plan next steps for their instruction and determine new learning targets. Because many students select books that are too easy instead of those appropriate for their reading level, the teacher designs a focus lesson that teaches her second graders how to recognize when a text is too easy for them, and then teaches a strategy for selecting a just-right challenging text. As these teachers provide targeted instruction and feedback to students, they slowly begin to see the independent-reading lives of their students and their classroom environment changing.

In this example, establishing independent-reading practices in their classrooms is a necessary first step before students can learn how to prepare for and engage in a discussion because the text used during independent reading provides the content. These teachers know that the students' stamina to read books they select based on reading level or interest free them to work with individuals and small groups. Besides, their students are able to immediately apply and practice these newly taught strategies directly in their independent-reading text.

As these second-grade teachers learn more about their students and have the rituals and routines of independent reading firmly established, they begin to design other focus lessons to prepare students for student-led discussions. Their next focus lessons include establishing group norms and generating and asking questions to move the discussion along. Group norms could include:

- Be respectful of all
- Give everyone a voice
- Be present
- Listen

Generating questions include:

- Creating teacher-generated questions first and then expanding to student-generated questions
- Understanding and using open-ended questions
- Developing questions while reading and while in discussions

These second-grade teachers are amazed at the transformation, engagement, and excitement for learning in their classrooms when they put students in charge, give them choice, and empower them to talk about books. They can't wait to incorporate student-led discussions in their instructional practices more often.

As it relates to this book, this process's most essential element is for students to engage in authentic conversation. It sparks interests, clears up misunderstandings, provides new ways of thinking about important ideas, and generates new questions. A great conversation includes students presenting ideas and citing evidence from a variety of texts, answering open-ended questions they generated, encouraging all voices, listening attentively, and responding to others' ideas to broaden understanding and construct new learning.

Chapter 3

# TAKE ACTION!

Build opportunities for students to strengthen relationships by talking with one another in positive, respectful, productive ways. Choose one activity, analyze your classroom for one week, and make a list of what you and what your students are doing in each lesson. How are students engaged and how might you use this information to adjust your lessons moving forward?

| Date | Learning Target | What the Teacher Is Doing | What Students Are Doing |
|---|---|---|---|
| | | | |
| | | | |
| | | | |
| | | | |
| | | | |

chapter 4

# Experimenting With Different Discussion Formats and Strategies

*Discussion with other kids helps motivate me. If you have a teacher standing in front asking questions, most kids aren't going to raise their hands and think. But when you are in a group discussion, you have to say something—you get your ideas out.*

—AUSTIN, grade 9

You're inspired to jump in and begin your journey by providing the conditions, time, and space for student-led discussions that you read about in chapter 3 (page 43). You know the recipe and ingredients to invigorate student learning through dialogue among students using the framework chapter 2 (page 15) describes. You can take the next step by putting those elements together along with a discussion format that fits with what you are already doing in your classroom. In this chapter, we offer a variety of discussion formats teachers can incorporate into their lessons. Consider the following example as a way to include different structures to help students understand content.

A class may begin with a *think-pair-share* about a question related to the learning target that sparks student thinking and creates additional questions as well as answers. This format allows a student to think about a topic individually before they pair with a partner and discuss what each person is thinking. Then, they pair with a partner and discuss what each person is thinking. Finally, the teachers ask student pairs to share their ideas with other students in the class. After generating interest, the teacher delivers explicit instruction with modeling in a *focus lesson* and may use a shared reading, video, or audio clip to provide background knowledge while further stimulating student interest in the topic.

Next, students select or receive a text that aligns with the learning target. As they read the complex text, they may stop at various spots and talk with a partner using a discussion format to better comprehend the selection. Later, they may *apply their learning* and deepen their understanding even more by engaging in a debate or small-group discussion in which the teacher *observes*, *records notes*, and provides individual as well as group *feedback*. Finally, students *reflect* on their personal and group development. Note that these activities may occur over the course of a few days, depending on the length of your class period or focus of your work.

This chapter spotlights myriad discussion formats you can apply in all content areas, which we more fully explore in chapter 5 (page 87). Think of the discussion formats as building blocks that lay the foundation for a variety of communication strategies to take place, creating support and motivation for students to engage in meaningful academic dialogue. When you couple these discussion formats with the student-led discussion framework from chapter 2 (page 15), you establish a vision, complete with tools for transforming learning in any classroom.

## Choosing a Discussion Format

You might think that engaging students in robust discourse that develops language and the capacity to reason in a content area may be overwhelming, if your instructional methods are more teacher led. Although this feeling is perfectly valid, there are some very basic discussion formats you can quickly and regularly learn to use regardless of your current skills, academic expertise, or grade level.

Often classroom discussions take one of two forms—either (1) we ask questions and students respond in a question-and-answer format or (2) students are given the opportunity to turn and talk to a partner about a concept, topic, or idea (Fisher et al., 2008). Although both methods are useful, adding to your instructional repertoire provides variety and enhances student engagement.

Knowing, then, that we want to increase the opportunities for student classroom discussion, you can include different discussion formats during your instruction, depending on your learning targets. Table 4.1 provides an example of three discussion formats and different strategies for each format and its purposes.

**TABLE 4.1:** Summary of Discussion Formats

| | Turn-and-Talk | Partner Chats | Small Groups |
|---|---|---|---|
| **Purpose** | Student shares thoughts or ideas with a partner for thirty to ninety seconds. | Partners discuss a topic in depth for longer periods of time. | Four to six students discuss a topic or talk about text or texts to understand multiple perspectives. |
| **Strategies** | • Think-pair-share<br>• Inner- and outer-circle | • Exchange diaries<br>• Say something<br>• Blogging | • Student-led discussion groups<br>• Inquiry groups<br>• Book clubs<br>• Debates<br>• Jigsaws |

Each format has strengths and confines for developing students' understanding of content as well as their speaking and listening skills. Teachers can use most with any grade level. Elementary, middle, and high school learners all benefit from implementing multiple discussion formats. By purposefully selecting the most effective format for a specific learning situation, you take advantage of the oral and written communication skills that each variation provides. Besides, students learn in a variety of ways. What works for one student may not produce the same results for another. By varying the discussion formats, you increase the chance of matching different learning styles to the diverse makeup of your students.

Written discussions are often more personal and give students a chance to express themselves in a nonthreatening way. Students tend to write more about themselves, their beliefs, understandings, and struggles when they are initially given the opportunity to share in a more private way. Written discussions often reveal an individual's level of understanding through his or her feelings about a topic. Discovering ways for these written discussions to occasionally go public—in order for others to read and respond—builds confidence, motivates learners, and develops students' online discussion skills. The knowledge you gain from reading student writing can guide your instruction while also providing information about next steps for students that can be used during individual conferences.

Partner dialogue is the most-used technique in classrooms and can be very effective. You may ask students to turn-and-talk, think-pair-share, or journal back and forth while reading or discussing text. In each format, students build relationships and trust with one another—important qualities needed for robust conversations to occur. Moreover, they are a way to ensure all students engage in conversations about essential content rather than the select few who choose to participate.

Group discussions allow students to put their heads together, hear different perspectives, and develop deeper understanding. When students explain or defend their positions and their thinking to others, they discover the importance of speaking concisely with important details. Students become models for others. They watch effective modeling, listen and learn information, see new ways of thinking, and experience effective communication skills, which strengthen their own speaking and listening skills.

A group discussion is successful if multiple perspectives about a topic are shared, many good questions are posed and answered, and all students are attentive and involved. Undoubtedly, conversations promote more sophisticated thinking from our students and, more often than not, increase their motivation. Deep discourse is most likely to occur when groups of students work collaboratively to talk about meaningful content.

Effective instruction requires that we become intentional about every decision—selecting the appropriate discussion format and strategy impacts engagement, learning outcomes, and higher-level thinking. Students thrive on variety and novelty. Regularly adjusting the discussion format to a specific need or purpose piques students curiosity about what's coming next.

## Turn-and-Talk

Besides providing an opportunity for students to deal with a chunk of information they just heard or read, you can use the turn-and-talk discussion format in several other ways during a focus lesson. Some situations in which it works well include:

- As a warm-up activity to discuss a previous lesson or homework assignment
- As a quick formative assessment to get a pulse on students' understanding
- As a reflection activity before providing closure to a lesson

Since the purpose of the turn-and-talk discussion format is to provide frequent opportunities for short conversations, students may veer off topic or some may lose focus if the thirty- to ninety-second time protocol is not consistently applied or we don't provide clear directions and feedback. If losing focus during turn-and-talks, revisit and model for students what active listening looks like and sounds like, or provide question stems for students until they are able to generate them on their own.

Inexperience with the routines for talk often leads to our students' poor performance (Fisher et al., 2008). We need to remember that consistent inclusion of short bursts of dialogue among students results in stronger application. Therefore, structured opportunities to engage in frequent conversations using a strategy like turn-and-talk, and applying its protocols with fidelity, will engage students in dialogue while practicing the routines for talk before expanding the group size beyond two participants.

When you begin a lesson with a question that allows for equal access, all students can contribute to the discussion, regardless of their academic and language abilities. After posing the question to the group, use the turn-and-talk method to engage and involve students in the beginning discourse about the topic. Should all U.S. citizens be required to complete a year of community service? and When is it okay to lie? are two questions that provide equal access. These types of questions should link directly to the learning target and are often used at the beginning of a focus lesson to set the environment for student-centered learning.

Although turn-and-talk is a quick and easy way to get started with student-led discussion, it can become routine and students just go through the motions instead of applying new thinking and fully attending to the discussion. The more variations of the turn-and-talk format that you put in your toolbox, the more options you have for keeping discussions fresh, new, and engaging for all students. Table 4.2 describes two such variations: the think-pair-share and the inner- and outer-circle. By becoming more familiar with this format, you often invent new variations and apply them in novel ways.

Although quick turn-and-talk opportunities offer a solid structure for starting our students with purposeful talk, their scope is limited. Consider other discussion formats, like those you'll read about through the rest of this chapter, when the goal is to engage students in deep discourse.

| Strategy | Description | Benefits |
| --- | --- | --- |
| **Think-Pair-Share** | Students think about an idea for a short period of time. They share their ideas with a partner, each taking turns talking and listening. A few pairs may share with the whole class. | This collaborative learning strategy is best used for quick, structured conversations to solve a problem or answer a question. It works well in focus lessons or during guided practice. |
| **Inner- and Outer-Circle** | One circle of students sits inside another circle of students facing each other. Each student in the inner circle is paired with an outer circle student. A question is posed and pairs respond. At the signal, one circle rotates one position to form new partners. | Inner- and outer-circle is used mostly for short discussions. Students have opportunities to work with many different people. |

**TABLE 4.2:** Turn-and-Talk Discussion Format

## Partner Chats

When you want students to tackle an idea, discuss another point of view about an issue, or scrutinize a problem, you need to give them more time to talk with a partner. We use the term *partner chats* for these sustained, partner discussions. This term signals that students will be given more time to dialogue with a partner. Video 4.1 "Grades 1, 7, and 2: Partner Chats" shows an example of students in first, second, and seventh grades engaged in dialogue with their partners. It reinforces the importance of partner chats to elicit additional thinking from students, strengthen understanding, and give all students a voice in discussion.

Like turn-and-talk, the partner chat discussion format involves half of students in talk at any one time. By participating in a conversation with a partner, pairs are given opportunities to dialogue, expand on ideas, challenge a partner's perspective, and listen attentively. Table 4.3 describes three types of partner chats.

| Strategy | Description | Benefits |
| --- | --- | --- |
| **Exchange Diaries** | A notebook is shared between two people, whereby pairs take turns writing and responding to their thoughts or comments about their reading. | Journal writing benefits students by enhancing reflection, facilitating critical thought, allowing them to express their feelings, and letting them develop focused arguments. |
| **Say Something** | Students say something to a partner at various points while reading a text. They can generate a prediction, ask a question, clarify an idea, make a comment, or develop a connection. | Say something requires students to become active during the reading process and share their thinking with diverse partners. It engages learners and provides an opportunity for them to respond and build on ideas to broaden their understanding. |
| **Blogging** | A regularly updated webpage is maintained by an individual or group and written in an informal or conversational format. Blog entries might include information, commentary, or media such as videos or graphics. | Blogging integrates technology and gives all students, especially those more reluctant to speak up, a voice when sharing and responding to each other. Because of its informal structure, blogging serves as a great way for teachers and students to get to know and better understand each other. Blogging improves student writing skills and increases the volume of writing in any classroom. Students are engaged in purposeful writing for real audiences. |

**TABLE 4.3:** Partner Chat Discussion Format

Your role differs from the turn-and-talk situations while students are talking in pairs. Partners using this discussion format spend more time talking; therefore, you should observe, take notes on what they are saying and doing, and use these notes to provide individual or partner feedback.

In this section, we talk in more detail about exchange diaries and about the say something strategy. You can learn more about blogging later in this chapter, in the section, Talking Chips: Helping All Students Speak and Listen Equally.

### *Exchange Diaries*

Exchange diaries are an informal way for students to engage in a written conversation about a topic, text, event, or situation. These short writing activities give students a chance to think and respond to a question or information another student shares. Going public is often intimidating. Exchange diaries and other strategies that encourage students to write before speaking can be the gateway into stronger discussions. English learners or less proficient students need time to think or jot ideas on a topic prior to initiating discussion (Mohr & Mohr, n.d.). In our observations, these same learners often benefit from talking with others before engaging in more formal writing; doing so often sparks ideas, broadens vocabulary, and allows for questions to be asked and content clarified. Students who are more reluctant to speak up in class or during discussion aren't without opinions and information worthy of hearing. We just may need to vary our approach if it's not working for some students.

### *Say Something*

Say something is a discussion strategy used to help students comprehend text while reading, because deriving meaning from a story, article, or passage is difficult if readers wait until the end. You can use say something with any genre or excerpt and it is easy to model for students. Posting and responding to questions, making comments, and paraphrasing are some speaking and listening skills exercised while using this strategy.

Although we provide a sixth-grade example of this discussion format, the strategy works with all grades. As students engage in this strategy, you observe, listen, and later provide feedback about their use of listening and speaking skills in addition to the content they discussed. When students are partnered up using this strategy, you can only listen to one group at a time. Therefore, you may need another form of reading response, if you want to know what individuals understand and think about the text.

Modeling the say something strategy during a focus lesson with a short text is essential. Ideally, it works best to model the strategy with a colleague when using the technique with younger students, or with a communicative student or older student. Beforehand, the modeling pair should read the text together and prepare an example of each response students might use—making a prediction, asking a question, or generating a connection.

In figure 4.1, the teacher shares the learning targets for the say something strategy during the focus lesson. In the example that follows, Ms. DeAngelo, a sixth-grade teacher, models the use of this strategy with a colleague.

| Learning Target—<br>Reading | Learning Target—<br>Speaking and Listening |
|---|---|
| I can think deeply about a text to determine the meaning of words and phrases by making predictions, asking questions, providing comments, or generating connections in at least three different places within the reading selection. | At least three different times during our discussion, I can pose and respond to specific questions with elaboration and detail by making comments that contribute to the topic, text, or issue under discussion. |

**Figure 4.1:** Using the say something strategy.

Ms. DeAngelo says, "Today we are going to learn a new strategy, called say something, that we can use during reading. The say something strategy engages us in conversations with a partner several times as we read through a text.

"To apply this strategy, we might stop at the end of a paragraph when reading a complex text, after each stanza of a poem, at the end of a section when we read informational text, or when we finish a number of pages in a novel or picture book. We stop at these places to discuss a point we find powerful or interesting, to clear up any confusion we have about the text or content, or to ask a question to help clarify our thinking. We read many different types of text and this strategy can be used with any genre."

Write the directions on an anchor chart and post on the wall or provide a handout or bookmark with directions to help students. See figure 4.2 for the anchor chart.

**Say Something Strategy**

1. With your partner, decide who will say something first.
2. When you say something, do one or more of the following.
    a. Ask a question.
    b. Clarify something you might not understand.
    c. Make a comment.
    d. Develop a connection.
    e. Generate a prediction.
3. If you can't do one of these five things, then you need to reread.
4. Your partner should comment on what you have shared by doing one of the following.
    a. Answer your question or ask a follow up question.
    b. Make an additional comment or connection.
    c. Help clarify the content or meaning.

**Figure 4.2:** Anchor chart of say something strategy.

The teacher states, "We are going to practice using the say something strategy with the poem *Still I Rise* by Maya Angelou. I have asked Mr. Ibarra to model the strategy with me, and then I will share my thinking about the first two stanzas. Finally, you and a partner will finish reading the poem while using the strategy to enhance your understanding.

"Remember, poems are often best understood with multiple readings, so don't hesitate to reread it when necessary. It also helps to understand the context in which the poem is written to help you make inferences and grasp the underlying meaning. Maya Angelou wrote this poem in the 1970s, just after the height of the civil rights movement. It was a time when many African American people broke into mainstream American jobs, but there was lasting resentment and anger that stretched back to the 1800s and the time of slavery. Watch and listen for how we apply the say something strategy to better understand the meaning of this poem."

Ms. DeAngelo reads one stanza as it is projected for students. Then she and Mr. Ibarra talk about it before reading the second stanza. Ms. DeAngelo says, "When the author says 'bitter, twisted lies,' she sounds really upset or sad about the way people have described her. Despite her bitterness, she sounds resilient when she says, 'But still, like dust, I'll rise,' like she can overcome anything."

Mr. Ibarra agrees, "When she uses the words dirt and dust as she talks about what people are saying it reminds me of sticks and stones."

Ms. DeAngelo reads another stanza. She comments, "She has a lot of confidence and seems wealthy when she says, 'Cause I've got oil wells pumping in my living room.' Do you think most African Americans were as confident as she was?"

Mr. Ibarra asks, "Is she really confident or just putting up a front? You can hear the attitude and emotion in her voice. I think she is tired of racist comments and actions and is finally taking a stand. You can see by the imagery Angelou creates that she is a descendent of slaves and is tied to that history and struggle. In the eighth stanza, she writes about rising from huts of shame, from a past rooted in pain. It is this allusion to slavery that Angelou uses as a backdrop to her poem that celebrates the gifts she has been given and the role racism played in attaining her strength to persevere."

Ms. DeAngelo says, "Now, I want to review how Mr. Ibarra and I used the say something strategy. I first used the strategy to make a comment about a couple of phrases I found intriguing. Mr. Ibarra responded by making a connection between the words dirt and dust to sticks and stones. The second stanza led me to my question where I wondered if all African Americans had confidence, followed by Mr. Ibarra's question and his statements to clarify the content.

"How does the use of this strategy help us better understand the poem?" (*Waits for responses.*) The teacher goes on to say, "As you can see, this is a descriptive poem that will give you and your partner much to think and talk about. Remember to stick to the guidelines of say something. The first person begins by saying something to which the partner responds. Reread when necessary and be sure to use this (*points to anchor chart*) to help you when you get stuck."

Connecting one person's ideas with another's ideas may be a difficult concept to teach but will enhance and deepen student conversations. In the first conversation, Mr. Ibarra just says he agrees with Ms. DeAngelo before rushing forward to communicate his thoughts. Whereas, in the conversation about the second stanza of the poem,

Mr. Ibarra challenges Ms. DeAngelo's thinking by posing a question and linking his next thought with what his partner just said.

Students need to learn to build on a partner's thoughts or ideas and appropriately confront them. Although this concept is important, it is often not practiced during turn-and-talk opportunities because of the exchange's brevity. Partner chats, including say something, allow students time to address, connect to, or respectfully challenge a partner's point of view before moving to a larger group.

Early in the school year, when you are working to build relationships among your students, we believe it makes sense to vary partnerships often. But, by matching students with specific partners for an extended amount of time, students' trust with one another builds and stronger discussions occur. With purposeful modeling, consistent use and feedback, students come to understand and value this strategy.

## Small Groups

Some content is better addressed using a small-group discussion format. Yet, these small-group, student-led discussions take more time than when we present the content through a lecture format or even a partner chat. So, how do we know when a particular instructional format is worth the time invested?

Consider four questions that may help guide your decision as to whether the small-group discussion format works best for helping students understand the content.

1. Is this content essential information that all students must understand, thus worthy of spending additional time?
2. Are multiple perspectives needed to understand this content?
3. Could various approaches be applied to understand this content?
4. Is the content so complex that having students talk together might help clarify meaning and deepen understanding?

When you answer affirmatively to any of these questions, small-group discussions may be a highly effective tool for students to learn and retain important content. Table 4.4 (page 68) illustrates three strategies for this discussion format.

We cover student-led discussion groups and inquiry groups in more detail next. You will read about more detailed examples of using the debate strategy in the section Using Multiple Concurrent Discussions, later in this chapter.

### Student-Led Discussion Groups

Student-led discussion groups create opportunities to increase dialogue among students, strengthen speaking skills, and use academic vocabulary. To showcase student-led discussions here, we use video 4.2 "Grade 3: Using Informational Text for a Student-Led Discussion," which includes a group of third-grade students talking about an informational text they read about unsolved mysteries. Video 4.3 "Grade 4: Using Discussion to Tackle a Challenging Mathematics Problem" features fourth-grade

**TABLE 4.4:** Small-Group Discussion Format

| Strategy | Description | Benefits |
|---|---|---|
| **Student-Led Discussion Groups** | A group of students meets to discuss a text or texts they are reading, or a concept or event from a specific area of study, such as social studies, science, or mathematics. | Student-led discussion groups improve comprehension for students because they experience productive ways of thinking about text. Small-group interactions with peers offer several benefits, such as practicing context-relevant speech and reducing anxiety. |
| **Inquiry Groups and Book Clubs** | An inquiry group formulates a question or questions to guide learning. The members apply information, look for results, reflect on their learning, and perhaps even challenge the validity of a text or an idea in light of contradictory results that come from their own direct experience, careful observation, and analysis.<br>In book clubs, students talk about a book they have all read to gain deeper understanding of the content and consider other points of view about the book. | Inquiry groups take increasingly greater risks with more time and practice together which builds a repertoire of skills and strategies. Students learn from each other's successes and mistakes.<br>Through book clubs, students develop important language skills, make predictions and solve problems; and book clubs provide students with opportunities to try out new vocabulary words. |
| **Debates** | A debate is a formal, disciplined, competition that is conducted using a defined structure. A debate may comprise individuals or teams that include several students. | Debate helps students see the power of utilizing rational, reasoned arguments and compelling evidence. It teaches them the skills of researching, organizing, and presenting information in a compelling manner. |

students involved in a mathematics discussion, illustrating collaboration, persistence, and stamina while solving difficult problems in mathematics.

Students begin using discussion as a vehicle for learning rather than using it only for informal communication. They comment, question, and learn how to invite all members into the conversation as well as share information or argue for a different solution to a problem. Speaking in a group requires practice. The best way to positively impact student learning and to accelerate their vocabulary acquisition, as well as their speaking and listening skills, is to provide frequent opportunities for students to practice.

### *Inquiry Groups*

Inquiry groups work together through an exploration, experimentation, and discussion cycle to discover answers to their questions, learn more about their world, make connections, and share their learning with others. Some might argue that the inquiry approach to teaching isn't suitable for our youngest learners; however, these learners are inquisitive (Gordon, n.d.). They ask questions and test out their theories as they go about their day.

In the first-grade classroom example that follows, see figure 4.3, Ms. Garcia works with students to understand and utilize the turn-and-talk format in September and October. In November, much less prompting is needed, and after that it becomes a norm in the classroom culture. During that time, inquiry groups are also used in language arts, social studies, and science to help students strengthen their skills. Inquiry groups start out with partner activities before expanding to triad groups for these early learners.

| Learning Target—<br>Social Studies | Learning Target—<br>Speaking and Listening |
|---|---|
| I can look for ways and come up with one way to make the school community a better place. | With my partners, together we can select one way to make our school better and tell our classmates. |

**Figure 4.3:** Using the inquiry group discussion strategy.

Students in this first-grade example have been exploring roles and responsibilities as citizens in a school community. Before this focus lesson, students also learned about the various roles, responsibilities, and rights of different staff members by interviewing them and recording their findings on a classroom chart. Now students are ready for Ms. Garcia to begin this lesson.

She says, "Remember when we talked to Mr. Benton, our custodian at Rahn Elementary, and asked him questions about his roles and responsibilities that help make this a better learning community? He shared with us that his most important role at school is to keep us safe and provide a clean environment. He also told us about some of his responsibilities, like helping with tornado and fire drills, setting up for school events, shoveling the sidewalks, vacuuming in classrooms and hallways, and assisting lunchroom staff. In your role as students in the Rahn community, you also have the responsibility to make your own classroom and school community a better place.

"Let's think about Dr. Suess's *The Lorax* (1971), our interactive read-aloud from the last couple of days. The Once-ler didn't think about or listen to others. He was only thinking of himself when he cut down all of the Truffula Trees. His actions destroyed the environment for everyone else—the Swomee-Swans, Brown Bar-Ba-Loots, and the Humming-Fish. If the Once-ler had been responsible like Mr. Benton, his environment would have been a safe, clean space.

"Just like Mr. Benton and the Once-ler, you have responsibilities here at school. You are going to work in a small group of three people to explore and identify ways you can make our classroom or school community a better place. In just a minute, we are going to walk around the building—through the hallways, the lunchroom, the media center, and on the playground. During our walk, you and your group will draw or write down observations as you look for spaces and places to help keep safe and clean." Teacher and students take a walking field trip around the school.

"During our walk, I saw many of you write and sketch different ways that you could make our school community a better place. You will now work together within your group to discuss the things that you wrote or sketched during our walk. As a group, you must agree on one way to make our school a better place."

Amelia says, "The halls were dirty. Look, I drew a picture of a bunch of winter stuff that was lying in the hallway on my whiteboard. See, I drew jackets, boots, and mittens."

Preston says, "I saw that too, and I saw paper towels and papers on the floor. People are littering in school."

Calvin asks, "What is littering?"

Preston responds, "Littering is when people throw garbage on the ground instead of in the garbage cans. We need everyone to hang up their stuff. How can we get kids to clean up?"

Calvin says, "Student council can help us and talk to everyone. We could make a video to show the problem and teach kids how to clean our school."

Amelia explains, "That's a good idea, Calvin. Someone could dress up as the Once-ler, throwing boots and mittens on the floor in our video just like how the Once-ler cut down the Truffula Trees in the story."

Preston adds, "Everyone else in the video can help clean up and talk to him to show the right thing to do."

Conversation continues for a short amount of time and the teacher brings the group back to the whole group to facilitate closure by sharing the new ideas they came up with and connections made to the text.

Following this lesson, students spent chunks of time writing, drawing, or recording (or all of the above) the steps and materials needed to make their school a safe, better environment over the next few days. Then, they share their work with the rest of the class. Finally, the class selects one or more ideas and actually makes the improvements at the school.

One student triad decides that the Rahn Elementary community would be a better place if all students and staff in their school would compost food and recycle plastic and paper products correctly. They make a few posters, illustrating food, trash, and recycling that should go into each bin in the lunchroom.

After brainstorming as a class how they can help everyone remember the importance of recycling, Ms. Garcia's students decide to ask the lunchroom staff to hang their posters up to help teach and serve as a reminder. Paired with these illustrations, students use an iPad to produce and record a short demonstration video of two students discarding the remaining items left on their lunch trays. This video is then shared using Google for Education's YouTube channel (www.youtube.com/user/eduatgoogle), posted on the teacher's classroom website, and sent out electronically as a link for all school staff and families within the school community.

Consider the learning tasks and choice given to students during this inquiry. Although it would have been much easier for Ms. Garcia to just write a list of ways to help around school, students now own their learning and have taught themselves and others how each member of the school community has a responsibility to keep it clean and safe. Students don't forget when they are engaged in this type of learning—they are thinking, talking, making decisions, and collaborating (Gordon, n.d.).

Each classroom of students is unique and has different needs. The different discussion formats are not meant to be a checklist or a comprehensive recipe of how to facilitate deep academic discourse in classrooms. However, they can provide the variety needed to get our students comfortable with purposeful talk.

## Using Alternate Discussion Strategies for Different Purposes

Your purpose drives the discussion format you choose for your students. When designing instruction, select the best instructional strategies needed to engage students and facilitate their mastering the learning target. Turn-and-talk is an excellent discussion format to use during focus lessons as they provide time for students to have quick, structured conversations that may elicit background knowledge, share their thinking, or challenge an idea or opinion.

Partner chats have similar features to turn-and-talk, however, make sure you allow students to engage in conversations that can be richer and more meaningful. Students build trust in partnerships, which shapes confidence. This assurance is great not only for students' self-esteem but it also strengthens the classroom community necessary for collaborative, and possibly controversial, conversations to occur.

Small-group discussions encourage a broader understanding of multiple perspectives about a topic (Fisher et al., 2008). Student questioning, responses, and inquiry propel small-group discussions. In this format, our students become leaders in conversation, engaging in rich dialogue about important content. We observe that during small-group discussions students assume responsibility for their learning while teachers observe and use feedback to guide and advance all students' understanding.

Each discussion format has a place in classrooms at various times. A language arts teacher will spend a great deal of time teaching communication and presentation skills during class. In contrast, a content-area teacher will briefly touch on these skills but remain more focused on history, biology, or other subject areas. If students discuss content in conjunction with hearing information teachers present, they will make deeper connections that enhance their understanding. Equally important, while students are engaged in these discussions we are free to observe, listen, take notes, and confer with groups or individuals about specific behaviors they are or are not exhibiting. Feedback done in this manner is timely, relative, and specific—a structure where students and teachers can thrive. No matter the content area or grade level, students need to talk far more than they are listening—in partnerships and small groups.

Sometimes conversations among students break down or don't work well for a variety of reasons and some formats work better than others depending on the purpose or learning target. For example, students may not listen attentively to another person and the conversation is like popcorn in a popper moving from one student to another without making direct connections among comments and dialogue. The protocol for the say something strategy specifies what options students have after the student makes a comment that may help address this issue.

Another thing that may happen is that a few students may dominate the conversation while others sit passively without contributing. The talking chips strategy, which we describe in more detail later in this chapter, works well to focus on balancing the contributions among all group members.

*Fishbowl* is a strategy that invites students to be both contributors and listeners in a discussion with an inner circle and one or more outer circles. It is structured so that an outer circle of students can observe while the inner circle of students engage in a discussion. The inner- and outer-circle strategy explained later in the chapter differs from fishbowl in that all students are paired with one student for discussion and rotate partners every couple minutes. Its purpose is to give students frequent opportunities to talk with different, varied partners.

During fishbowl, viewers in the outer circle note particular look-for elements that need attention to assist their peers in moving forward with their speaking and listening skills. As the outer circle observes and takes notes, students in the inner circle construct meaning, analyze a text, connect responses to others, cite textual evidence, or sustain a conversation. Its purpose is to permit the outer circle to be observers of discussions and give meaningful feedback to their peers.

Sometimes teachers use the fishbowl strategy to demonstrate skills they want other students to know and use during their discussions. The unpredictability of what students might say, how long it takes them to demonstrate the highlighted skill, and whether they model the particular skill effectively informs us that the use of video clips to highlight particular skills often works better for demonstration purposes (Novak, 2014a). We can be assured that the skills we are hoping to illustrate will actually appear in the discussion.

When you offer students a variety of structured discussion formats, you prepare them for self-directed conversations. You may start with a simpler and more structured format and add more complexity and less support as students move along the continuum to independence. As you become more familiar with the discussion tools and the results they yield, you are able to select a discussion format that matches the learning need.

## Talking Chips: Helping All Students Speak and Listen Equally

Introducing new content in mathematics is typically done by step-by-step demonstrations of some sample problems, using the question-and-answer format with students along the way (Stigler & Hiebert, 1999). Yet, a growing body of research indicates student engagement in meaningful mathematical discourse has a positive effect on students' mathematical understanding as they increase the connections between ideas and representations (Cirillo, 2013).

Mr. Washington, a third-grade mathematics teacher, wants his students to have opportunities to talk in small groups, but his most astute mathematicians are dominating the conversations. He selects the talking chips strategy to help address this need (see table 4.5).

**TABLE 4.5:** Talking Chips Discussion Format

| Strategy | Description | Benefits |
|---|---|---|
| **Talking Chips** | Each student is given the same quantity of chips. When a student wants to say something, the student places a chip on the table. No one is allowed to speak unless a chip is placed on the table. After a student uses all his or her chips, the student's only participation option is as an attentive listener within the group. | Talking chips are used to promote equal participation within a group. This strategy also could be used with individual students who dominate a discussion but the number of chips given to the student should be determined in consultation with the student to prevent a negative outcome. |

The talking chips strategy ensures all group members get equal opportunities for sharing, enhance group communication skills, and provide shared practice of learned language as well as application of new vocabulary in context. Engagement is critical to student success and the talking chips strategy increases participation from all students. More reluctant speakers develop their conversation skills and active communicators listen to others more closely, think before responding, and learn to monitor the frequency of their responses. The talking chips strategy allows students to make use of their communication skills while helping them become more attentive facilitators of their own learning.

As you work with your students, you need to explicitly teach content and deepen their understanding by letting them talk in whole group, small group, and with partners. Although the mathematics example that follows, beginning with figure 4.4, uses the talking chips strategy to facilitate student learning of a problem-solving strategy in third grade, it can be used effectively in any grade or subject.

| Learning Target—Mathematics | Learning Target—Speaking and Listening |
|---|---|
| I can determine the meaning of a mathematics problem and explore more than one way to solve it. | I can explain the technique I used and my thinking about how to solve a mathematics problem. I can then listen and respond to questions about my solution. |

**Figure 4.4:** Using the talking chips discussion strategy.

Mr. Washington models a problem-solving strategy and explains the talking chips discussion technique during this focus lesson. He says, "Today's learning targets are (*shares and points to the learning targets posted on the board*). When solving a problem in mathematics we ask ourselves some questions after reading a problem. What do we know? What are we trying to figure out or answer? Which of the following problem-solving techniques should we use to find a solution?" Mr. Washington reads from an anchor chart that was generated in a previous focus lesson, such as make a table or graph, find a pattern, draw a diagram, and so on.

"Remember, there isn't one right technique to use when solving a math problem. Choose the one that works best for you. After solving today's problem, we are going to use a new discussion strategy called talking chips. During this activity you will listen and respond to others after they have explained their process and solution to the problem. You will also have the opportunity to share how you solved the problem with others.

"Talking chips is a strategy we will use several times throughout the year because it gives each of you a voice when sharing or responding to others during a discussion while encouraging you to really listen closely to what others are sharing. Since we know there are several different techniques we can use in math to solve most problems, sometimes we can learn about these different strategies from others. Here are the directions for talking chips." (*Mr. Washington shares the full details of the talking chips strategy.*)

"Let's look at the following mathematics problem: Your uncle gave you a gift certificate for $50 and you want to try to spend every penny! Your choices are a movie pass that costs $12, an arcade pass for $14, and a recreation pass costing $22. What will you buy to come as close as possible without going over the $50 your uncle gave you?

"I am going to share how I might approach the problem. First, I think about the problem I am trying to solve then I proceed with finding a solution. Listen for the technique I use and the combination of passes I choose to get closest to spending the $50 gift certificate. (*Pauses*)

"I have been given $50 and need to find the best combination of passes that I can buy so that I have as little money as possible when I'm done. I just identified the problem I am trying to solve. Next, I need to determine a technique I will use to find a solution so I am going to create an organized list of all possible combinations.

"Well, I think I will try to purchase one of each pass: $22, $14, and $12." Mr. Washington writes the numbers on the anchor chart. He then says, "Forty-eight dollars is close to my target, but I am going to try again to see if I can spend exactly $50. I think I will try a different approach to get closer without going over $50. If I get four movie passes the total will be $48." He adds this combination to the anchor chart. (See figure 4.5.)

| Recreation Pass $22 | Arcade Pass $14 | Movie Pass $12 | Total Spent |
|---|---|---|---|
| 1 | 1 | 1 | $48 |
| 0 | 0 | 4 | $48 |

**Figure 4.5:** Problem-solving activity.

Mr. Washington asks, "As you have heard, I talked about my thinking as I tried to come up with a combination that equals exactly $50. What did I try first?" (*Waits*) "What thinking did I do after my first attempt fell slightly short of spending my entire $50?" (*Waits*) "I am wondering if there are other solutions and different ways to solve this problem so I need your help to see if you can figure out a combination that will spend the entire $50," he says.

Next, Mr. Washington asks students to think about another combination to spend the $50 gift certificate. Then, he asks students to pair up and share the combination they each discover. This guided practice provides Mr. Washington with data from a quick formative assessment whereby he can determine if his students understand the task before releasing them to independent work time.

He says, "You can work this same problem independently, choosing a different problem-solving technique to come up with a solution. After that, you will meet in small groups and use the talking chips strategy to share and discuss your methods and solution to this problem."

Students are given time to work independently on the problem. Next, the teacher assigns students to their triads. The conversation that follows is from one group.

Amari places her chip on the table and begins explaining how she solved the problem. "I made a number sentence," she says. "I subtracted $22, the cost of the recreation pass, from $50. The number sentence looks like this." (*She shows her whiteboard to the group.*) "Fifty dollars minus $22 dollars equals $28 dollars. I know that $28 is equal to two arcade passes, which are $14 each, making a grand total of $50. My new number sentence reads $22 plus $14 plus $14 equals $50."

Placing his chip on the table, Jack says, "You found a different combination than Mr. Washington and the way you came up with it was different! See?" (*Jack points to the anchor chart created during the focus lesson.*) "He said four movie passes. In your solution, Amari, you didn't even include a movie pass. I wonder if it's possible to get exactly $50 without using an arcade pass."

Placing his chip on the table, Will says, "I don't think it is possible because each movie pass is $12. One equals $12, two equals $24, three equals $36, and four equals $48. None of these are $22 (the cost of the recreation pass) so it can't total $50."

After time elapses and students have shared techniques to solve the problem. Amari places a chip on the table and asks, "What do you think is the best way we used to solve it?"

Will places another chip on the table and responds, "I liked the list that Mr. Washington made because it was easy to see the totals, but I think Amari's way of using a number sentence is faster."

Jack places another chip on the table and adds, "It might be faster, but the list that Mr. Washington made would make it easier to see and find all of the possible combinations. Should we see how many different combinations we can make to spend $50?"

After about ten minutes, Mr. Washington notices that all students have had a chance to use their chips at least once and most students have solved the mathematics problem using a variety of techniques. He then gathers the whole group together to provide closure to the lesson and prompt students' thinking.

Examples of prompts from the teacher include:

- What different methods of solving the problem did you learn about as you listened to your group members?
- What are some examples of the responses given after group members shared their explanations?
- Hold your thumbs up if everyone in your group had a chance to share something with group members.
- How did it make you feel when you shared with the group? How did it feel as a listener?
- Talking chips is a strategy we will continue to use. What is something you liked or were good at during this activity? What is one thing you would like to work on and do better next time?

Mr. Washington's students are more likely to experience success because he effectively modeled both the discussion format and his approach to solving the problem. Important ideas in mathematics are developed as our students explore their own solutions to problems, rather than being the focus of instruction (Cai & Lester, 2010). Their excitement for this type of instruction is evident by one group's response, when it found a combination of passes to use all of the money. In unison members shouted, "Mr. Washington, Mr. Washington! Come look! We used two different techniques and both ways let us use exactly $50!"

Talking chips is a low-risk activity for students, one that teachers can use in any classroom at any time during the school year. Students might discuss their strategies and solution to a mathematics problem, the experiment results in science, how a character's actions contribute to a story's plot, or a school issue your students are assigned to problem solve together. Talking chips helps students learn about their strengths and areas of growth as speakers and listeners. Yet, the artificial restraint of equal representation of speaking opportunities doesn't align well with real-life application. Therefore, its use should be limited to highlight the importance and value of each member's contributions to the group.

Reasons that talking chips is a particularly effective strategy for mathematics are because the Common Core mathematics call for conceptual understanding of key concepts and emphasize using multiple representations to connect various approaches to a situation in order to increase student understanding (NGA & CCSSO, 2010c). The focus lesson used in the example provides multiple strategies and models for those representations to introduce, explore, and reinforce mathematical concepts and deepen conceptual understanding. The strategy allowed every student in the group an opportunity to speak and respond to the problem they were trying to solve.

Discussions help students to be clear, convincing and precise in their language, enabling the use of higher-order thinking skills that are critical elements of mathematical discourse (National Council of Teachers of Mathematics [NCTM], 2000). NCTM encourages us to use discourse in our mathematics classes to support both students' ability to reason mathematically and their ability to communicate that reasoning. The NCTM's (2000) *Principles and Standards for School Mathematics* speaks to the need for students to make conjectures, experiment with problem-solving strategies, argue about mathematics, and justify their thinking.

As we'll explore even deeper in chapter 5 (page 87), learning to reason well is important in all subjects, but it takes practice. When students engage in discussion, they share their reasoning with others and respond to their peers' reasoning. Thus, we give students the practice they need by using talk in strategic ways. By committing to teach for understanding in mathematics, we must allow discussions to be a key component of our instruction.

## Blogging

Some of our most quiet and reserved students rarely talk, so you might want to use another strategy to engage them in dialogue with their peers. Blogging is a form of discussion through writing to enhance student interaction and learning. We provide students with a safe environment to share their ideas, make comments, publish work, and demonstrate their learning. Using blogs produces several benefits. Blogging, or online journaling, gives all students a voice and lets them learn and collaborate with an authentic audience while using critical- and analytical-thinking skills and accessing quality content (Martin, n.d.). Since it isn't a formal process, it allows students to express their opinions, interact socially with peers, and support their thinking through a freestyle format without getting bogged down by the rules of writing. It also provides an authentic audience and offers opportunities for immediate feedback.

Although blogging isn't a new idea, some reluctance from teachers to try this effective strategy may result due to the lack of knowledge about its many benefits or the lack of computers in classrooms. One solution is to expect students to read, post, or respond to a blog once or twice a week using any device in or out of the classroom. Blogging can be used for many purposes. We might use blogging to communicate school or classroom news to students and families. We can also post a comment or question that challenges students' thinking, promotes debate, or causes them to reflect on their learning. Ideally, students will shift from just responding to others' questions, comments, and posts to contributing and facilitating their own online discussions.

One reason we may hesitate to use blogs in our classrooms is that we may have reservations about having our students' conversations made public for everyone to see. Yet blogs can be private and classroom based, with only the class's enrolled students able to view and contribute. Or, they also may be public and accessible to anyone online. A public site creates a broader sense of audience and participation that may embody a global community. It's important to take precautions if the site is public. Students' posts should be monitored closely and parent consent may be required depending on district policies. The book *From Pencils to Podcasts* (Stover & Yearta, 2017) highlights platforms, including blogs, that teachers can use in classrooms without the risks of being totally public.

Blogging is an excellent tool to support our students' reading and writing lives. Figure 4.6 illustrates how Ms. Shahad, a ninth-grade language arts teacher, set up the use of the blogging strategy in her focus lesson.

| Learning Target—Reading | Learning Target—Writing |
|---|---|
| I can determine a theme or central idea of a text and analyze in detail its development by identifying at least three details evidenced in the text. | By posting one blog entry and responding to the blog posts of at least two others, I can use words or phrases to identify the theme and link it to supporting evidence to show its development. I will respond to another blogger's idea and evidence by agreeing, challenging, or commenting. |

**Figure 4.6:** Using the blogging strategy.

Ms. Shahad says, "You have been reading *To Kill a Mockingbird* the past couple of weeks. Today, I want you to go back into your notes and select one of the central themes you identified in the text that interests you, and then identify a portion of the text that illustrates that theme. Your blog post must include a direct quote or small excerpt from *To Kill a Mockingbird*, the development of the theme with supporting details you have selected, and a question for readers. When you respond to a classmate's blog, you should make a comment, ask a follow-up question, provide other examples that support the theme suggested by the first blogger, or offer another idea for a theme with your own rationale.

"To meet the learning target, each person is responsible for posting one entry and responding to at least two other blogs. We have examined themes before so keep these in mind as you write your review."

The teacher then displays examples of exemplar blogs where students identify a theme, support it with evidence that details its development over the course of the text, and another blogger responds. Finally, students are released to begin their independent work. In the following example, the student begins writing with a quote from *To Kill a Mockingbird* (Lee, 1960), as illustrated in figure 4.7.

As each student adds a comment or question to the blog post, other students join the conversation. Some students may be extremely quiet in class; yet, they may be more likely to comment on a blog. Students who have spent very little time together in school may become connected, and blogs allow students to become experts in the area they are posting.

Often, student questions in a blog promote more engagement than could have been accomplished through a class discussion. Follow-up responses from an initial post result in new questions, deeper understanding, and increased passion about the topic. Blogs give students time to process and think about their comments, allowing for deeper and richer conversations and debates. With more time to think and reflect, students advance their thinking, beyond simple recall, to analyzing and synthesizing information. Blogs encourage experimentation and risk taking and may foster an increased awareness of private and public writing. Students may use this discussion

> Hush your mouth! Don't matter who they are, anybody sets foot in this house's yo' comp'ny, and don't you let me catch you remarkin' on their ways like you was so high and mighty! Yo' folks might be better'n the Cunninghams but it don't count for nothin' the way your disgracin' 'em—if you can't act fit to eat at the table you can just set here and eat in the kitchen! (Lee, 1960, p. 26)

The student then continues, "*To Kill a Mockingbird* encourages us to examine our morals and ethics. In this excerpt, Calpurnia's moral lesson is to respect individual differences even if we think we are better than someone else. According to her, acting like we are better than someone is the surest way to show that we are not. This text supports the stereotype that white people have morals but African Americans do not.

"In the United States, respecting differences in people is a journey we have been on for over one hundred years. How do our actions today perpetuate this problem? And how do the ways we treat people now compare to the way people were treated in the 1930s?"

**Figure 4.7:** Sample student blog post.

format to learn at a distance and communicate at any time, not just within the boundaries of the school walls and the school day.

In addition to blogging's benefits, remember your purpose for its use. In this example, Ms. Shahad wanted her students to determine a theme and describe its development in the text by citing evidence. Whereas, the student did provide textual evidence to support the theme she suggested, the question she raised takes the attention away from the text.

NGA and CCSSO call on us to use discussion and writing prompts that focus on the text to build a strong foundation of knowledge (as cited in Thome, n.d.). Focusing just on the theme from details in the text is a fourth-grade standard for reading, whereas noting how the theme emerges, is shaped, and refined by specific details across the text ratchets up the rigor to a ninth-grade level. A type of question that this student could have asked during the discussion to keep other students in the text might be, "What examples have you found from various parts of this book to support *To Kill a Mockingbird*'s theme that different morals exist for white people and African Americans?"

## Using Multiple Concurrent Discussion Strategies

In the age of computers, we have experienced exponential growth in access to information. Coupled with increased access to information, most teachers feel they can't possibly cover all the academic content in a given subject. Therefore, what our students know becomes less important than what they can do with their knowledge.

In the following high school example, a variety of discussion strategies are used before students engage in a student-led discussion where they create new knowledge to solve problems. Ultimately, Ms. Keller, the science teacher, wants students to know how various environmental issues impact the sustainability of human societies.

In this unit, students learn content by listening, reading, and talking, and are given many opportunities to work with partners and small groups through experiences that include: using jigsaw, creating a summary and sharing it with their inner- and outer-circle partners, debating an issue, and finally discussing in small groups how international environmental problems impact the sustainability of human societies.

First, Ms. Keller uses a focus lesson to introduce six environmental topics to students. For this particular lesson, she wants students to learn about some international environmental problems. Therefore, she selects the subtopics: (1) spread of invasive species, (2) wildlife trafficking, (3) global warming, (4) pollution, (5) changes in ecosystems, and (6) ozone depletion.

## Jigsaw

Ms. Keller wants students to make an informed choice of which topic they want to study more extensively, so she uses the jigsaw strategy to share a significant amount of content through an expedited process (see table 4.6).

**TABLE 4.6:** Jigsaw Strategy Format

| Strategy | Description | Benefits |
|---|---|---|
| **Jigsaw** | The jigsaw strategy is an efficient way to learn a significant amount of material in a short time. Students are placed into small groups where content to be learned is divided and assigned to each group member. They each become experts through close reading about the topic or section of text and then discuss and share key information with others. Upon completion of the jigsaw, students are experts on one topic and knowledgeable about all. | Each group member plays an active role during jigsaw, through reading, synthesizing, sharing, and listening. When done, students will have learned the most significant information presented in the entire text. The experts in jigsaw groups provide a support system for students, while learning about various topics or issues. Jigsaw promotes deeper understanding and success for all and is an excellent strategy for students to apply group process and communication skills. |

The seven steps of the jigsaw process work as follows.

1. Divide students into five- or six-person jigsaw groups, diverse in terms of gender, ethnicity, reading level, and other factors, to explore a central topic.
2. Identify six subtopics for exploration.
3. Each jigsaw group member selects from the six subtopics with each member reading about a different one. The teacher gathers and distributes a two-to-three-page overview document on each subtopic. (Reading resources should contain differentiated instructional levels for all members of the class to access the content.)
4. Students read about their chosen subtopic, take notes in the margins, mark the text, and highlight key points.

5. Form temporary expert groups by having one student from each jigsaw group join other students with like subtopics. These expert groups discuss the main points of their overview article and take notes on important ideas to bring back to their jigsaw group.
6. When students return to their jigsaw group, they present their new learning to their group.
7. As a group, members then decide which subtopic they want to explore more deeply.

Figure 4.8 illustrates an example of a science-based learning target that could be explored using the jigsaw process.

| Learning Target—Science | Learning Target—Speaking and Listening |
|---|---|
| I can explain how one international environmental problem may impact the sustainability of human societies. | I can contribute key information about my subtopic; listen; synthesize the comments, claims, and evidence others present; respond thoughtfully to diverse perspectives; and collaborate to determine the next steps required to deepen our investigation. |

**Figure 4.8:** Using the jigsaw strategy.

Students need multiple opportunities to work with and develop the underlying ideas. The appreciation of those ideas and breadth of understanding develop over a period of time, rather than a class period or a few days. Therefore, the discussion format description that follows typically occurs after students have been given time to dig deeper into the topic.

Students continue to work in their original jigsaw groups expanding their knowledge on their subtopic. After students independently research their subtopic and find four relevant resources, at least three of which are text based, they read, watch, or listen to the information presented, making notes about key ideas.

As an example, one group chooses to explain how wildlife trafficking may impact the sustainability of human societies. The students divided the tasks to learn deeply about this environmental issue. Research topics include:

- What is wildlife trafficking, where is it occurring, and what costs are associated with this problem?
- How does wildlife trafficking occur?
- What controversies exist with wildlife trafficking?
- What are some problems and examples of wildlife trafficking?
- What can be done to prevent it?

Students need to read and research their segment of the topic before their group work in order to thoroughly explain how wildlife trafficking may impact human societies' sustainability. Students explicitly draw on evidence from text and other research to stimulate a thoughtful, well-reasoned exchange of ideas. During discussions, students make new connections, pose relevant questions, and clarify or elaborate on others' ideas. Through this jigsaw activity, students respond thoughtfully to diverse perspectives while working together in a collaborative group, much like real scientists' work. Ultimately, students tackle the overarching question: How does wildlife trafficking impact the sustainability of human societies?

## Inner- and Outer-Circle Partners

After the collaborative group wrestles with this problem, it needs a way to consolidate members' thinking and reveal their personal knowledge about the topic. Each student writes a short summary about the key components of the information shared during the group discussion, ensuring the individual accountability important to successful collaborative learning. This written reflection also promotes further synthesis and translation to long-term learning.

Using the inner- and outer-circle strategy, each inner-circle student presents a summary to an outer-circle partner. When signaled, the inner circle rotates one position and each student shares his or her summary a second time with a new partner. After the two partner discussions conclude, the inner-circle students share their new learning while outer-circle students listen, take notes, and later extend the conversation when the roles are reversed. This exchange solidifies students' understanding and allows them to practice using concise language, and their summarization skills, in an authentic experience.

## Debate

To apply their learning about the environmental issue they studied, students *debate* a controversial current event related to their topics. The group that chose to do an in-depth review of wildlife trafficking decided to debate the question: Should Walter Palmer, the man who shot Cecil the lion in a national park in Zimbabwe, Africa, be fined and prosecuted?

Recall a *debate* is a structured process with the purpose of learning how to argue effectively. Each team makes an opening statement to the audience where it states its position, evidence, and reasoning. After both sides have completed opening statements, each team has a designated amount of time to prepare a rebuttal. Rebuttals address one or more specific arguments the other team makes with evidence or reasoning. Debates give students opportunities to identify specific texts that support and defend their position and to listen to other students. They nurture critical-thinking skills, develop metacognition, and facilitate reasoning and students' ability to share viewpoints with others.

Literature also highlights key benefits of debate as a teaching and learning strategy for developing critical-thinking and analytical-thinking skills while fostering teamwork and communication (Snider, n.d.). Debating demands all students are actively involved and responsible for learning. Additionally, it provides an experience by which students can develop competencies in researching current issues, preparing logical arguments, actively listening to various perspectives, differentiating between subjective and evidence-based information, and formulating their own opinions based on evidence.

There are some cautions about debates you should keep in mind. Sometimes students can influence others' thinking without being accurate. This distorts learning. Also, some issues have multidimensional viewpoints that may be better addressed in an open discussion.

### Problem Identification and Solving

This culminating student-led group discussion determines similarities and differences among various environmental issues, resulting in a synthesis of their impact on human societies. Students propose actions that could be taken to solve these problems. When students create new knowledge to solve problems they help identify, they practice the "single most important skill that all students must master today" (Wagner, 2012, p. 142).

In this final activity, new student groups form, which comprise one member from other groups that studied different environmental problems—spread of invasive species, wildlife trafficking, global warming, pollution, changes in ecosystems, or ozone depletion—to broaden students' perspectives about other environmental issues. Armed with more information than the first discussion, conversations evolve into deeper, richer discourse. In other words, students generate, sustain, and learn from true student-led discussions.

## Understanding the Benefits of Multiple Discussion Formats

The high school example in the Using Multiple Concurrent Discussion Strategies section includes a variety of discussion formats to engage students in meaning-making about important content. Students paid attention to facts presented from multiple texts. They were taught and held accountable for the content and to one another. And they learned techniques to keep the conversation flowing toward a richer, deeper understanding of an important topic. Through these discussions, students needed to take initiative to think critically, be resourceful, and communicate effectively. These experiences developed students' confidence to explore, question, test, experiment, and push the boundaries of relevancy. These are important skills for students to master and valuable tools for later life in a rapidly changing world.

Moving discussions from conversations to deep discourse takes time. It begins with creating a strong, safe community where we engage students with meaningful texts and activities. When our students are given frequent opportunities to collaboratively study, share, and talk about their learning in this type of environment, using various discussion strategies, their inquisitive minds are nourished. Chapter 6 (page 105) explores even more ways to enable students to communicate effectively.

## Chapter 4

# TAKE ACTION!

Use this reproducible to apply your learning and, potentially, as a springboard for professional development work.

1. Select a discussion strategy you have not tried before and use it with your students. Ask students to provide feedback about what worked well and what they feel needs to be done differently the next time it's used.

Select one discussion format from the following list:

- ☐ Turn-and-talk
- ☐ Partner chat
- ☐ Small group

Select a strategy you used from the chosen discussion format and share what went well and what needs to be changed.

| Strategy | What Worked Well | Changes Desired |
|---|---|---|
| | | |

2. Anticipate three challenges that might occur as you implement this and other discussion strategies. Brainstorm specific steps to take in order to alleviate or overcome each challenge.

**Challenge 1:** ______________________

Action steps to overcome challenge:

**Challenge 2:** ______________________

Action steps to overcome challenge:

**Challenge 3:** ______________________

Action steps to overcome challenge:

chapter 5

# Using Discussion in Different Content Areas

*If you don't understand the math work, homework will be really hard. When you're in small groups, someone can explain it to you so you understand.*

—BRIN, grade 7

We often associate student-led discussions with literacy-based classes. However, as we touched on in chapter 4, understanding and retention of material increases significantly in *all* content areas when the presentation of content is mixed with frequent opportunities for students to talk. Therefore, all educators must be open to opportunities for students to learn from others through discussion.

The classroom culture impacts how freely students engage in discussion. Welcoming and inclusive classroom cultures promote collaborative learning where students are encouraged to take risks and make mistakes while teachers provide feedback and allow revisions. In these schools, the emphasis is on student growth and understanding while still paying close attention to student achievement.

Students who experience discussion demonstrate higher levels of thinking and increases in student achievement (Applebee, 2003; Murphy et al., 2009). Yet, in order to maximize cooperation's benefits, and ultimately promote learning, students must understand how to work together, contribute, accept responsibility for completing their part of the task, and help others learn in a supportive environment (Frey, Fisher, & Everlove, 2009; Johnson & Johnson, 1990, 2006; Slavin, 1995).

## Engaging Different Views of Learning

So, what does it sound like in classrooms where the focus is on learning through mistakes, collaboration, and persistence? Consider the following exchange in which a student is supposed to explain how he tested his hypothesis.

Mr. Paz says, "Tomah, explain to the class how you tested your hypothesis."

Tomah replies, "I don't think I can say what I did."

Mr. Paz says, "If you explain how you thought through building your design, maybe we can help you figure out the pieces you are missing. As you think aloud, we might be able to help you figure it out."

The messages Mr. Paz sends inform the students in the classroom that sharing their thinking is an opportunity to learn and that learning is a collaborative process in which all students participate. Having students expand on their responses is often most difficult for our strongest learners who instinctually know the answer and are accustomed to just moving on. By increasing expectations for students to explain their answers, we boost the rigor of a seemingly easy task. "When teachers help students build on their thinking through talk, misconceptions are made clearer to both teacher and student, and at the same time conceptual and procedural knowledge deepens" (de Garcia, n.d., p. 2).

## Teaching and Learning by Content Area

As subject-area teachers, we are content experts. Although difficult, we are also responsible for showing students how to read, write, and discuss topics about our subjects. Through this important work, students learn to read and respond to content like scientists, historians, and mathematicians.

The examples this chapter outline infuse content into the framework for student-led discussions. We highlight three different content areas—(1) mathematics, (2) science, and (3) social studies—and also share *why* using the framework to guide instruction will help your students make great gains.

### Mathematics Example

Each subject has different methods or processes for learning content. For example, students can come up with answers to several mathematics problems independently, or you can present students with real-world problems and opportunities they can use to inquire, collaborate, problem solve, discuss, and reflect on their new learning. As students learn new concepts, their understanding solidifies through discussion. If your focus in mathematics is limited to a right or wrong answer, then you have also limited student thinking and prohibited them from applying their learning to new situations. In thinking about mathematics, you want students to be able to demonstrate and share the *how*, or the process of learning and solving a problem. As they continue to explore mathematics concepts, they will forge connections and begin to understand *why* their answers work. Consider the following learning targets and focus lesson.

**Mathematics learning target:** I can calculate the area of triangles and parallelograms (square, rectangle, and rhombus).

**Speaking and listening learning target:** I can work collaboratively with my partner to solve a mathematical problem through creativity, discussions, and revisions with a final persuasive presentation of my proposal.

Let us illustrate two different approaches to a sixth-grade focus lesson about finding the surface area of triangles and parallelograms. In classroom A, Mr. Barrett presents the mathematics learning target, which he also posts on chart paper, to his students.

**Focus lesson:** Mr. Barrett then quickly draws the three different shapes. He models the use of each formula, sharing his thinking with the class as he solves each problem. Occasionally, he asks students to determine what formula he used to solve the problem, or to provide him with a value for a variable in a problem. Once complete, students apply their learning independently by practicing several similar problems to those Mr. Barrett models. The next day's lesson follows the same format; however, students learn to solve the area of trapezoids or circles using different formulas. "Most classroom talk consists of the teacher lecturing, asking students to recite, or posing simple questions with known answers" (Chapin, O'Connor, & Anderson, 2009, p. 5). In this classroom, not all students are given the opportunity to practice the speaking and listening learning target.

Now, let's consider classroom B, which offers a different approach to the very same concept of understanding surface area. Although Ms. Flora works toward the same learning targets as Mr. Barrett, she extends the learning target to include a speaking and listening goal. Ms. Flora begins the lesson with a question, "Why are understanding and the ability to calculate surface area important or necessary for certain professions or in our daily lives?"

Immediately, students engage in a turn-and-talk discussion, generating answers to the posed question, thinking about the concept of surface area, and applying it to their daily lives. The discussion between students highlights several ways this concept is used and prepares them for the day's lesson.

This focus lesson is similar to Mr. Barrett's lesson in that Ms. Flora shares and models how to calculate the surface area of triangles and parallelograms, and has students practice a few examples with guidance. Unlike Mr. Barrett, she has students apply their new learning to a real-world problem. This *application of learning* is the bridge from a teacher-controlled style of learning to student independent learning and thinking.

Ms. Flora shares the problem students are to solve. She says, "Mr. Martin has purchased a new home with a large backyard measuring $x$. He wants to build or include the following three things in his backyard, yet maximize as much open space in his yard as possible: an $x$ garden, an $x$ patio with a fire pit, and an $x$ shed.

"For the remainder of today's class period as well as tomorrow's, you are to work with a partner to create and design a backyard plan that you believe is Mr. Martin's best option. During the middle of your project, you will pair with another group to share and discuss your work plans and also give and receive helpful feedback to consider as you move forward to complete your project. After you present your work plans and solutions to another group, and receive its feedback, you may want to make some changes. Feel free to make the changes before you present your final plans.

"The final plan must include a sketch of the yard to scale, with all perimeter and area measurements labeled clearly and accurately, equations, formulas, and calculations needed throughout your project, and a brief written pitch to Mr. Martin that explains, with evidence, why your design is the best option for his yard. Let's create a checklist together on this anchor chart so you are sure to have all the required parts of the plan for your final presentation. What do you need to include?" (*Pauses to solicit responses*) "Each group will present and discuss its plan with two different groups and, together, determine whose plan is best for Mr. Martin."

Questioning is a critical component in supporting students to engage in meaningful discussions. The NCTM standards address the important role questions have in the mathematics classroom. When students are working collaboratively to solve problems, we want them to rely more on themselves to determine whether something is mathematically correct. Therefore, the questions posed will advance their thinking to work through problems more purposefully. In order to assist students with their work, the teacher referred to some broad questions (table 5.1) hung from the ceiling and on pieces of chart paper posted around the room. These questions will help guide students' thinking, planning, and discussion.

**TABLE 5.1:** Questions Students Use to Develop Their Mathematical Thinking Skills

| Mathematical Thinking | Question Prompts |
|---|---|
| Determine the problem. | • What is the problem we are trying to solve?<br>• Why is this problem important?<br>• How is it similar to other things we have done? |
| Demonstrate mathematical reasoning. | • What do we need to do to solve the problem?<br>• What predictions can we make before we begin?<br>• What will we need to do to justify and explain our problem-solving approach and solution? |
| Organize data and draw conclusions. | • How can we organize our data?<br>• What conclusions can we draw? |
| Check results and correct mistakes. | • What mathematics principles did we use to design our plan?<br>• Do these results make sense?<br>• Is anything missing?<br>• How do we know this solution is correct? |
| Model and define new concepts. | • Do these conclusions pose questions for further exploration?<br>• What have we learned? |
| Make judgments and create proofs. | • Why do we think this is the best plan?<br>• What examples and counterexamples can we provide to support our reasoning?<br>• Is our proof logical?<br>• Is there any part of our proof that we cannot support with a rational argument? |
| Communicate problem and solution to others. | • How can we share our work of solving the problem along with our solution so it makes sense to others?<br>• What is the best method to communicate our findings? |

*Visit* ***go.SolutionTree.com/instruction*** *for a free reproducible version of this table.*

Students are calculating, creating, modifying, collaborating, engaging in partner discussions, evaluating, and conferring with other groups as they work toward mastery of the learning targets throughout the learning phase. In this case, they are focused on deeply understanding surface area and applying their new skills to a real-world problem in a collaborative setting. The guiding questions for both teachers and students, combined with *careful observations* of the mathematics discussion and student interactions, provide *data* that are used to pinpoint where students are in their learning and determine the next steps for growth.

The *feedback* that follows observing and recording data propels students and the teacher on their learning journey. When you expect students to respond to probing questions and feedback, they learn how to adapt new ways of thinking about mathematics. However, you must be sure that when you talk to students about their work, you go beyond giving them a number or letter grade—writing 8/10 on students' papers is not going to tell them how to improve their mathematical skills or what part of the problem-solving process they need to better develop. Telling them "Good job," or taking a quick glance at each student's work isn't going to help either. Posing good questions helps students think about, and then decide, whether they want to make any changes to their work. It is important that students know that they are the final decision-makers about what to do with the questions you pose and the feedback you give them. Table 5.2 provides examples of the type of questions the teacher might ask to propel students' thinking using the mathematical broad topics described earlier.

**TABLE 5.2:** Questions the Teacher Poses to Stimulate Students' Thinking

| Mathematical Thinking | Question Prompts |
|---|---|
| Demonstrate mathematical reasoning. | • Can you create a different shape to maximize the yard's space?<br>• What adjustments might you need to make to the perimeter of your garden to maximize space for a patio?<br>• Currently, you have all three items placed together in one area. Where might you place the garden or shed in order to create a pleasant view of the yard when I'm relaxing on the patio? |
| Organize data and draw conclusions. | • What knowledge about how the space would be used helped to draw your conclusions? |
| Check results and correct mistakes. | • What variables might you have to consider in your plan? Are you able to walk or mow around specific items? |
| Model and define new concepts. | • How would your design change if you had to plan for a family of ten with children under the age of eight?<br>• How might your design change if you are planning a backyard for an elderly couple? |
| Make judgments and create proofs. | • Why is this design the best possible solution for Mr. Martin?<br>• What evidence do you have that Mr. Martin will like your design? |
| Communicate problem and solution to others. | • Your backyard plan has all of the necessary items and labels. When I listened to your pitch to Mr. Martin, I was not convinced that this was the best plan. How can you reword your presentation pitch to sell your idea? |

The last step in carrying out the framework is for students to *reflect on their learning*. Too often, we skip over this part because we run out of time. Whether students respond to a prompt in their notebook, post a statement to your class blog, or begin the next day's class with a quick discussion with a partner, reflection brings the lesson and intended learning full circle. It allows students to self-assess their understanding by being aware of their thinking, articulating their learning, and making decisions about where to go next.

Throughout the mathematics lesson, students were engaged in many discussion formats—turn-and-talk, partner chats, and small groups. You'll notice that we used discussion strategies, such as jigsaw or say something that we covered in the previous chapter, but weren't specifically called out in this example. Although it is important to provide students with ample opportunities to talk and share their thinking using myriad formats, it is not our purpose to try to use *all* discussion formats in a unit of study. As you begin planning your lessons, you should try to provide a variety of ways to engage in purposeful dialogue.

In this example, students are involved in a turn-and-talk discussion format during the initial question and focus lesson activity. Because students worked together with one other student, partner chats took place throughout the entire problem-solving process: to talk about their initial plan, as adjustments needed to be made along the way, and when they began to analyze their design in terms of sight lines, efficient use of space, and how well it fit into the overall design of Mr. Martin's backyard. Lastly, there were two opportunities given to students to participate in discussion with small groups. Midway through the project, group members listen, share, and receive specific feedback. Their final discussion in small groups give students the opportunity to persuade others, share the strengths of their plan, and compare and contrast their plan with others. Table 5.3 summarizes and provides rationale for the different ways students were able to share with partners and in groups.

**TABLE 5.3:** Discussion Formats Used in Mathematics Lesson

| Turn-and-Talk | Partner Chats | Small Groups |
|---|---|---|
| • To determine prior knowledge and see how it connects to the real world<br>• To stimulate independent thinking about the mathematical concepts<br>• To increase engagement with the topic<br>• To prepare students for further discussions (prime the pump) | • To plan, model, design and reason to support decisions<br>• To make adjustments to their design plan based on small-group feedback<br>• To determine rationale for their design and contend why their design was the best mathematical plan for Mr. Martin's backyard | • To explain designs to another partnership midway through the lesson<br>• To present their pitch to two to three different groups and determine best aspects of their design<br>• To work together to select the best overall design for Mr. Martin's backyard |

A fundamental goal around mathematics instruction should be to develop a practice that respects the integrity of mathematics as a discipline as well as students as mathematical thinkers (Ball, 1993). With this goal in mind, we go beyond the boundaries of what is typically considered mathematics and include developing a culture in which students engage in conjecture, experiment, build arguments, and frame and solve problems, which mirrors mathematicians' work.

This type of work can best be accomplished when students are given many opportunities to dialogue together with partners and in small groups. And, as a student so aptly explains, "Sometimes it helps to hear kids explain how mathematics problems are solved because you hear it differently from the way the teacher explained it." Hearing multiple approaches to arrive at a solution builds students' repertoires of problem-solving strategies. You can watch examples of a fifth- and a sixth-grade mathematics discussion in videos 5.1 and 5.2 "Grade 5: Critical Thinking and Problem Solving in Mathematics" and "Grade 6: Solving Mathematics Problems Using a Variety of Strategies."

## Science Example

Inquiry is important in science education (American Association for the Advancement of Science, 1993, 2001a, 2001b; National Research Council, 1996, 2000). Yet, as science educators, we still grapple with what inquiry looks like in diverse classroom settings, the kinds of instructional experiences and practices that can best position students for inquiry learning, and what curricula to use that supports the development of science content and practices (Anderson, 2002).

The National Research Council's report on teaching and learning science in K–8 classrooms offers a perspective that emphasizes using and applying knowledge in the context of scientific activity (Duschl, Schweingruber, & Shouse, 2007). According to this view, students are more likely to advance in their understanding of science when they have opportunities to participate in science as practice. This science-as-practice perspective brings together content knowledge and process skills in an interconnected way (Lehrer & Schauble, 2006). Students experimenting and talking collaboratively together, in small groups, are conditions that support students' reasoning around conceptual issues and complex problem solving.

As educators, we might be challenged by knowing how much guidance or independence to give students. A proper mix of challenge and support might entail activities that help students understand how to think as they engage in tasks as well as how to procedurally do them, how to collaborate with classmates, and how to critically reflect on their learning (Davis & Miyake, 2004). This support requires our attention to their needs, which changes from a great deal of support to much less as students become more adept in their thinking, planning, and performance.

Ms. Schilling, a fifth-grade science teacher who is teaching a unit on bridges, uses *inquiry* in her teaching. Her instructional practices serve as an example of what is possible when a teacher understands students' thinking and uses that understanding to guide her instruction. A portrait of Ms. Schilling's classroom also reveals how her knowledge of science and pedagogy influence her instructional decisions.

**Science learning target:** I can build two different types of bridges and determine a way to test which is stronger.

**Speaking and listening learning target:** I can collaborate with a small group to solve an engineering problem through creativity, trial and error, evaluating possible solutions, and presenting our learning to others.

**Focus lesson:** Ms. Schilling begins the focus lesson by informing students they have been and will continue to study bridges to understand how bridges are constructed, their importance, and how their designs vary. She also describes how they will "talk like engineers," and then shares the learning targets.

She gives them materials after providing a number of visual examples of bridges followed by a brief explanation of their different structures. Next, she provides an inquiry challenge by asking them to use the materials to create a bridge that allows a toy car to drive across it like a real car might travel across a bridge that connects two roads.

As the teacher moves among groups, she notices one group of students has placed its piece of cardboard between two books on one side and between two books on the other. This design will not permit a car to travel on a connecting road. Therefore, Ms. Schilling reiterates the directions and asks the follow-up question, "Would a real car be able to travel across the bridge with a connecting highway on both sides?" She is careful to coach students to higher levels of thinking without interjecting her assessment.

When the students respond that a car could move across the bridge, Ms. Schilling asks a student to use the toy car to show her. By physically and unsuccessfully trying to move the car from one end to the other, they immediately realize that the books are in the way, so they begin to brainstorm solutions. Rather than abort their idea completely, one student conjectures, "What if we raise the second book high enough for the car to go underneath, and use four straws to support each book? This will provide extra support for our bridge!" Posing a question to a group is often all that is needed to propel it to the next step, rethink, or rework an incorrect or incomplete task.

Although she may look passive to the outside observer, Ms. Shilling is an integral part of student application of learning. She observes group progress on solving the engineering challenge and uses data from her observations to provide feedback to move student thinking along. You will note that the framework for student-led discussions is fluid and interdependent. It is not a series of discrete steps, but rather a holistic approach with much interplay between application of learning, observation and record keeping, and feedback.

If students had simply been given time to work an experiment on their own, it is highly unlikely that they would have spent their time efficiently. Students might get stuck in attempting a solution to a problem and either give up or waste lots of time. Although it's true that sometimes students profit from errors and that making mistakes is not always time wasted, it is inefficient if a student spends most of the experimentation time using procedures that are not optimal for promoting skilled performance. Through this type of dynamic probing of students' thinking and understanding their misconceptions, Ms. Schilling helps them come up with ways to think differently to guide them into a more plausible solution without telling them their solution was incorrect. The feedback she gives through questioning helps students reflect on their learning and make improvement.

As students work in groups to solve problems, Ms. Schilling observes the various problem-solving strategies and makes mental notes of student groups who should present their work. Since this inquiry lesson is done in September, the rituals and routines aren't developed enough to allow Ms. Schilling time to manage written notes. Later, as students become more proficient with managing tasks, materials, and discussion, she will take written notes to help her better understand her students' needs and growth. Whether done informally or formally, this observation of student progress and the translation to feedback are critical to growth.

Ms. Schilling wants a variety of solutions presented so that students will have the opportunity to learn from each other—*student-to-student feedback*. Therefore, she selects the group with the beam bridge stuck between two books—a solution that was incorrect—to present. This allows her to initiate a discussion about a common misconception and highlight the way the group adjusts its design with new thinking. She also selects a solution that is more sophisticated than most students have used in order to provide an opportunity for students to see the benefits of such a strategy and their thinking. Both the presentations of solutions and the class discussion provide her with information about what her students know and her next instructional steps.

Realizing that whole-group class discussions often rely on the thinking from one or two students, Ms. Shilling uses a turn-and-talk format that she embeds in the whole-group discussions. Despite being the second week of school, Ms. Shilling has explicitly modeled this approach and practiced its integration leading up to this inquiry challenge. In other words, she makes it foundational in her science classroom. This midpoint discussion is used to refocus student thinking and create time for reflection.

After this short class discussion, students were ready for their next inquiry challenge: "Using the materials you have, construct a different style of bridge using the bridge construction criteria—a toy car traveling on a road must be able to cross from one side to the other. After you construct your second bridge, determine which is stronger and then talk within your groups about your hypotheses. Be able to explain how you might know which is stronger," Ms. Schilling says.

For this scientific inquiry, students collaboratively make hypotheses and think about how they might test their predictions. In many classrooms, students rarely have to think much about designing experiments to test their predictions. Typically, they only have to follow steps teachers give them. Though more challenging, this approach develops their critical-thinking and problem-solving skills while promoting understanding of this inquiry topic. Therefore, Ms. Schilling provides question prompts from each category to guide their work (table 5.4, page 96).

**TABLE 5.4:** Question Prompts for Science Thinking

| Science Thinking | Question Prompts |
|---|---|
| Clarify experimentation. | • What problem are we trying to solve?<br>• What is the purpose of our investigation?<br>• What is our prediction?<br>• How can we set up an experiment to test our hypotheses?<br>• What observations can we make? |
| Justify answers. | • What does the data from our observations tell us?<br>• What conclusions can we draw from the data?<br>• What evidence do we have to justify our solution?<br>• How will we communicate our findings? What will we say? What prompts might we need to share our work with others?<br>• Is our evidence clearly communicated? |
| Extend or apply ideas. | • How can our knowledge from this experiment help us with other learning?<br>• What new questions does this inquiry leave us wondering about that we could also explore?<br>• How does this investigation relate to the real world? |

*Visit **go.SolutionTree.com/instruction** for a free reproducible version of this table.*

As the lesson progresses, Ms. Schilling carefully choreographs the sequence and flow of activities in a manner that helps her students make progress toward understanding the key science ideas of bridge designs. Presenting accurate science ideas and providing motivating and engaging tasks are important, but students run the risk of missing key points or picking up discrete bits of information that cannot be easily recalled and put to use if the ideas and tasks are not woven together in a way that allows for fluid sensemaking (Bransford, Brown, Cocking, & NRC Committee on Developments in the Science of Learning, 2000).

Students also made progress toward the speaking and listening learning target. In the beginning of the year, Ms. Shilling focuses on a few key skills for effective small-group discussion success, such as listening to the speaker in the small group and building on one another's ideas. These students are beginning their journey toward independent student-led discussions and have the opportunity to develop these skills in their application of learning. Yet on the continuum from teacher-supported to independent discussion, they are closer to teacher facilitated than student led. In subsequent inquiries and challenges, Ms. Shilling will purposefully move students along this continuum.

In this lesson, it is evident that Ms. Schilling's involvement and effort are especially needed in managing discussions. As she moved among groups, she asks and promotes questions that help clarify observations or inferences, extended or applied ideas, justified answers, and generated new knowledge or perspectives, and helped her students monitor their own learning. Through her questioning, she models how students might use questions to promote small-group discussion. In later lessons, she explicitly links the questions she posed in that first lesson to questions that students will ask each other.

Early in the process, students may not show much familiarity with scientific forms of reasoning and communication of the scientific processes they use. First, they may not apply their understanding of the function of hypotheses or experiments in scientific inquiry in their response to questions. When Ms. Schilling asks students for their ideas about building a strong bridge, the students tend, with few exceptions, to respond with short, unelaborated responses, often using the material from the experiment without transferring it to real life. They say, "We could use more cardboard," or "We could move the books closer together." They are not yet able to use their small-group discussion to work toward clear explanations of their thinking and learning.

Second, the students' explanation to the question, "How would you know for sure which bridge is stronger?" is answered with explanatory responses that reiterated things they thought they knew: "Because two cardboards are stronger than one." As students learn to challenge one another's thinking in respectful and productive ways, they learn how to answer these types of questions thoughtfully, with clarity and elaboration.

In the example, Ms. Schilling guides and supports her students as they explore problems, develop hypotheses, and begin to think about designing experiments to test their predictions. Even though not all students are proficient in their practices early in the school year, a community of inquiring minds is beginning to develop throughout the classroom. Students share the responsibility for thinking and doing: they distribute their intellectual activity so the burden of managing the whole process doesn't fall to any one individual. This community of practice can be a powerful context for constructing scientific meaning. Video 5.3 "Grade 5: Science Inquiry and Discussion" portrays a fifth-grade inquiry lesson of students constructing bridges to test their hypotheses and determining solutions. This lesson occurs in the second week of school.

## Social Studies Example

When many of us recall our experience in history classes we flash to wars, dates, and facts that the teacher and the text deemed relevant. Yet, this view of history is radically different from the way historians see their work (Sandwell, 2005). Social studies is intended to "help our students develop their ability to make informed and reasoned decisions for the public good as citizens of a culturally diverse, democratic society" (National Council for the Social Studies [NCSS], 1994, p. 3). Classrooms designed to include inquiry naturally promote and develop the collaboration, decision-making, and problem-solving skills needed to be informed, contributing global community members. NCSS's (2013) college, career, and civic life framework indicates a predominate role that inquiry plays in the social science disciplines. It informs us that students should develop questions and plan inquiries, apply disciplinary concepts and tools, evaluate sources and use evidence, and communicate conclusions and take informed action. Applying the student-led discussion framework can develop all these skills.

Students thrive on exploring controversial topics, sharing personal opinions, and learning to see the world through perspectives similar to and different from their own. Let's visit a high school U.S. history class. Recently, students learned the details, events, and implications the Louisiana Purchase had in the United States. The teacher, Ms. Diego, uses the content knowledge gained during that unit of study during a focus lesson.

**Social studies learning target:** I can analyze a single historical event from multiple perspectives and connect how it affected relations with external powers and Native Americans.

**Speaking and listening learning target:** I can apply my previous learning about the Louisiana Purchase in a role-play simulation with a sustained discussion through the lens of my assigned historical figure or group.

**Focus lesson:** The ultimate purpose of this focus lesson is to prepare students to participate in a student-led simulation about the effect of a historical event on a group of people. She knows that she will use this structure in the study of future historical events, and she wants to give students the tools they need to fully participate.

Role-play simulations can be used with all grade levels as they feature discussion rich with analysis and evaluation. In Ms. Diego's classroom, students have read widely, written, and discussed the changing face of U.S. history that came with westward expansion, including the Louisiana Purchase, immigration, and the rapid expansion of slavery. She plans a role-play simulation for her students to incorporate the historical knowledge they have gained, and as an effective outlet and culminating activity.

During the focus lesson, Ms. Diego models how to incorporate historical facts and details from multiple perspectives while assuming specific historical roles. She pays particular attention to including the implications the event had on relations between the different participants, which ties to her learning target and ultimately the social studies standard.

Ms. Diego uses a variety of question prompts to help guide her as she develops critical thinking in her U.S. history students (table 5.5). She pushes students to higher levels of rigor and challenges their thinking by asking questions that demand analysis, evaluation, and synthesis of new information. She lets them talk, write, and construct engaging learning activities.

Ms. Diego begins her focus lesson with the *why*. She offers that if we truly aim to understand the positive and negative impacts of an event, and how it influenced our culture and communities, we must learn about and hear the perspectives of all involved. She shares that, many times, historical events are presented from the dominant culture's perspective, and we, as consumers of information, must continually and critically assess the author's viewpoint in historical accounts in order to make our own determinations.

She next assumes the role of Napoleon Bonaparte, the French leader who many call the catalyst behind the Louisiana Purchase. She creates the following list of talking points from his perspective of the Louisiana Purchase. She is explicit as she links their previous learning about the event to one specific perspective. She extends her thinking

**TABLE 5.5:** Questions to Promote Critical Thinking in Social Studies

| Social Studies Thinking | Question Prompts |
|---|---|
| Identify roots and multiple causes. | • What possible causes lead to the event?<br>• While alone each individual cause may not have brought about the larger event, but when combined, what was the impact of their synergy? |
| Can explain multiple perspectives. | • How does the event change when viewing it through different lenses?<br>• Why do some people see this event having a positive effect while others would say they were negatively impacted? |
| Explain how events are interconnected. | • How did an event affect one group's relations with another group?<br>• What alliances or tensions between groups did the event cause? |
| Understand bias. | • A historical event often changes depending on who is telling the story. From whose perspective is this event recounted and in what ways does it influence the bias?<br>• How does the conversation change when others are included? |
| Link past to present. | • Trace the historical event forward and find effects of it in our world today.<br>• How would our world be different if a particular event never occurred? |
| Evaluate decisions. | • Would you have made the same decision as (character name)? Explain your position with rationale from your new learning. |

to show how the Louisiana Purchase affected relations between the different factions. Students will use the talking points during the simulation.

- That land is treacherous and barren; we are running out of funds and the Americans are willing to give us money for worthless land in the wilderness.
- It is so far away from France it is useless to us—we can't collect taxes on it and enforce our laws.
- Selling it will give France the money it needs in the U.S. war against Britain.
- If the Americans are willing to pay $3 million for it, France should sell it now without another thought.
- It is more important to gain European supremacy than to get a stronghold in North America.
- France will never be able to control the native population who inhabit it.
- Europe is the world center, and France needs to establish control over Britain.

After modeling and thinking from one perspective, Ms. Diego releases students to apply this learning and create their own lists. She had previously formed student partnerships that she used to quickly group students into pairs. She assigns the following roles to partnerships: U.S. President Thomas Jefferson, French military leader Napoleon

Bonaparte, the Lewis and Clark Expedition members, U.S. pioneers, and anti-Jefferson Creek Indians. In this way, Ms. Diego uses a partner chat and gives students a brief amount of time to prepare comments and ideas from their assigned figure's perspective—their talking points, which help students prepare for a rich conversation. She listens and observes the partner chats while *recording* strong elements that she sees and hears, as well as misinformation. She will later use her data and observations to provide feedback to the entire group.

The application of learning continues when Ms. Diego creates larger groups of four to six students, composed of two or three partnerships representing multiple perspectives surrounding the Louisiana Purchase. Students engage in a content-rich, sustained discussion from their historical figure's perspective. Students reference their talking points and weave historical events into the small-group discussion simulation. The conversation's goal is to determine which groups or individuals the Louisiana Purchase benefited and which groups or individuals were harmed. Once again, Ms. Diego's primary role during the role-play simulation is to observe and record data aligned with the learning targets of analyzing an event from multiple perspectives.

Ms. Diego sees and hears most groups engaging in a sustained discussion, but notices one group in particular is connecting the talking points to the larger question of the effects that the Louisiana Purchase had on the different groups. Using this information, she creates her focus lesson and application of learning for the following day.

As the class period draws to a close she asks students to *reflect* on their learning by taking a few moments to write on the following journal prompts.

- How did the simulation and discussion about the Louisiana Purchase highlight the need to acquire multiple perspectives when studying both current and historical events?
- What new ideas or new learning do you have about the Louisiana Purchase or historical events in general?
- How did the simulation role-play discussion make history more accessible for you?

At the bell, she collects journals to peruse before finalizing her plans for the following day.

In her follow-up lessons, Ms. Diego uses her observations and data from the previous day to create her new learning target for speaking and listening. Students continue to work toward the primary academic learning target of: *I can analyze a single historical event from multiple perspectives and connect how it affected relations with external powers and Native Americans,* but she modifies the speaking and listening target to move students forward in their learning progression. She grounds her focus lesson around: *I can apply my previous learning about the Louisiana Purchase with a sustained student-led discussion connecting ideas to one another.* She explicitly teaches students to create sentences and phrases that connect a previous idea to the idea or perspective they want to share.

Ms. Diego offers an example: After Andrew, who is portraying Thomas Jefferson, says that he will stop at nothing to expand territory to open up trade routes and provide access for economic expansion, Cate, who is portraying a member of the Lewis and Clark Expedition, connects to the previous comment. She acknowledges that Thomas Jefferson and the U.S. government's ultimate goal is to open this new territory for economic gain, but also understands that to do this it will be her party's responsibility to befriend and work with the native peoples who already inhabit the land. "When we connect our new thinking to previously stated information, it creates a sustained conversation instead of a series of choppy statements," she says.

Ms. Diego challenges students to generalize this learning beyond the role-play simulation to other discussions they will undoubtedly have in her class this year. As they conclude their learning about the Louisiana Purchase, they engage in another student-led discussion to apply their new learning about connecting sentences and phrases in a sustained conversation.

Next, Ms. Diego challenges students to determine which groups or individuals the Louisiana Purchase benefited at the time and which groups or individuals it harmed, plus support their answers with textual evidence during discussion. Because this new topic directly links to the previous day's conversation goal, Ms. Diego is able to move forward because the preparation and prethinking has already been done.

The discussion continues with students participating and all students engaged in the activity. Ms. Diego has seen the application of the new learning target: *I can apply my previous learning about the Louisiana Purchase with a sustained student-led discussion connecting ideas to one another.* In closing the lesson, she provides a few moments for reflection and invites students to return to their original partnerships. The talking prompt to facilitate reflection is: *How did the simulation and discussion about the Louisiana Purchase highlight the need to acquire multiple perspectives when studying both current and historical events?* She allows students five minutes for a partner chat before asking three students to share an idea that provides closure to the experience.

By the end of the unit of study, students move from being passive spectators of the past to enfranchised agents who could participate in the forms of thinking, reasoning, and engagement that are the hallmark of historians. The teacher's own understanding of history allows her to create a classroom in which students not only master concepts and facts but also use them in authentic ways to craft historical explanations. Video 5.4 "Grade 9: A Social Studies Discussion" demonstrates a ninth-grade student-led discussion example.

## Putting It All Together

Studies of students' classroom discussions indicate that they learn to use systematic inquiry tools to think historically, mathematically, and scientifically (Bransford et al., 2000). Higher-level thinking and questioning are both ingredients for, and products of, classrooms that engage students in discussions that require them to analyze, interpret, and develop new ideas and learning about the content being discussed. Student-led discussions should occur regularly in all content-area classrooms because they engage students in higher levels of thinking and learning than we could provide through teacher-led activities. "The extent to which this potential is realized depends on individual teachers who embrace discussion practices and use them as vehicles for connecting disciplinary knowledge to the hearts and minds of students" (Walsh & Sattes, 2015, p. 11). All of our students in every content area benefit from discussion with their peers.

Classrooms need to be a workplace for learning and doing—a collaborative environment that expects students to develop theories, ask questions, and research answers that challenge them. They need to talk with their peers to glean new enduring understandings and insights.

Chapter 5

# TAKE ACTION!

Use this reproducible to apply your learning and, potentially, as a springboard for professional development work.

1. Determine how often your students have peer-led discussions in subjects other than language arts. Try to increase the number by one the next week.

| Week of ___________________<br>Number of student-led discussions: ___________________ | | | |
|---|---|---|---|
| **Subject** | **Teacher Led** | **Student Led** | **Changes Desired** |
| | | | |
| | | | |
| | | | |
| | | | |
| | | | |

2. Review the modeling you do before student-led discussions in content areas. What changes do you notice when the teacher explicitly teaches and models both content and speaking and listening learning targets?

3. Create a list of sentence stems that you post in your classroom or use for your reference to challenge students as they prepare for or participate in discussion. Use stems like the following.

   *Can you provide evidence to support your conclusion?*

   *What steps did you go through that led you to this answer?*

chapter 6

# Getting to Deep Discourse

*I feel like an inflated balloon filled with ideas about the book. After we have a book conversation, the ideas get filtered out and I feel better.*

—PETER, grade 5

It was the beginning of October, and Ms. Swanson had been explicitly teaching skills and strategies for her fourth- and fifth-grade students to engage in meaningful discussions. She explains to her class that having a deep discussion about text is like learning to play basketball. "First, you learn how to dribble, shoot, and make offensive and defensive moves in isolation during practice. Relatively soon into the season, your team plays a game of basketball where you need to apply all the things you learned," she says.

Ms. Swanson adds, "During the first few games of the season, you may not be very good. For example, the ball might hit your foot as you dribble down the court or the ball may not even touch the rim of the hoop when you take a shot. As you continue to practice, receive feedback, and apply the new techniques your coach describes, your skills improve. You begin to make improvements as a team as well as individually."

This same approach applies to developing communications and critical-thinking skills. Explanation, elaboration, evaluation, disagreement, and questioning are all forms of discourse (Fisher et al., 2008) students must develop. When they are able to mix together these and other sophisticated skills in a conversation of ideas they are able to get to deep discourse, which results in inherent understanding of content.

## Applying Skills During Discussion

We believe that rich discussions transpire when connections are made, ideas are supported with evidence, thought-provoking questions get asked, and each group member's participation and perspective are welcomed and challenged. Ms. Swanson explains, "Your conversations won't be flawless from the start. Together we will observe—watch, listen to, and analyze your discussions to determine current performance and progress in each skill necessary for powerful conversations to happen. At first when you have conversations with others, you concentrate on each part of your new learning about deep discussions. You try out these different skills when you communicate in your small group. Soon, with lots of practice, feedback, and application of the helpful advice from your other group members and teacher, your skills improve. You begin to communicate more effectively and you learn more about the text you are reading and discussing."

Narrowing the focus by working specifically on one skill during a discussion is a critical step to develop students' capacity to achieve deep discourse. When we concentrate and give specific feedback to individuals and groups about that skill, we help build their confidence, which frees their minds to put the new skill into practice.

## Discerning Talk From Deep Discourse

Table 6.1 provides a depiction of some differences between student surface-level discussion and deep discourse. In order to achieve expert-like conversations, many principles listed in the deep discourse column should be apparent.

**TABLE 6.1:** Difference Between Student Talk and Deep Discourse

| Student Talk | Deep Discourse |
|---|---|
| Students *explain personal ideas* about a topic. | Students *explain*, *elaborate*, and *build on the topic* by matching a thought or idea to their personal life, other texts, or to the world. |
| Students *cite examples from text* randomly without making direct, relevant connections to the topic or using the text to support a claim. | Students *quickly and easily find and support ideas and opinions with examples* from text, which add depth and clarity to the ideas. |
| Students *generate questions* to begin the discussion. | Students *come prepared with* as well as *develop spontaneous thought-provoking questions* to clarify, probe, or challenge ideas which expand topics to gain deeper meaning. |
| Students talk whenever they have an idea to share with *some members talking much more than others.* | Students are consciously aware of how often and how much each member contributes to the discussion; therefore, everyone takes responsibility to *invite a member into the conversation* when he or she has not spoken for a while. |
| Students offer little or no *regard* of other members' comments. | Students *offer positive comments to a partner or paraphrase* other members' ideas to clarify or show that the listener understands and is interested in their contributions. |
| Students engage in discussion without *knowing the purpose or drawing closure.* | Students stay *focused on the purpose* and draw closure by *stating items* on which *they reached consensus* as well as discussion points they didn't resolve. |
| Students present their ideas with little or *no opposing views* others offer. | Students *consider alternative perspectives* and ideas, support as well as challenge them, and choose the best one by agreeing on its importance or value. |

As students converse and share their perspectives, they expand their ideas, enhance their thinking skills, and learn to communicate effectively. Students engaged in deep discourse use a variety of skills all at the same time. For example, students may talk about whether citizens should be allowed to own and carry guns. As the conversation evolves, students listen to opposing views, offer rebuttals with convincing, credible evidence cited from reputable sources, paraphrase key information others share, evaluate proof other group members share, summarize items of agreement, and synthesize new learning into a changing schema.

## Discerning Skills by Grade Level

Students need healthy doses of explicit teaching, practice, and feedback to get their minds in shape for deep academic discourse. Deep discourse skills can be taught to, and applied by, students in any classroom, although the sophistication and degree to which they are part of students' discussions may vary. Examining how a benchmark progresses in K–12 standards will assist in determining each skill's rigor and level. The information attained during this process will inform your instruction.

Beginning in first grade, students are expected to be able to build on others' comments and ask clarifying questions in small- and whole-group discussions. Even these young learners need opportunities to prepare for the demands of the more complicated conversations the CCSS call for. Table 6.2 contains examples of statements using forms of discourse at the primary, intermediate, and secondary levels.

**TABLE 6.2:** Different Grade-Level Examples of Discourse

| Form of Discourse | Primary | Intermediate | Secondary |
|---|---|---|---|
| **Explanation** | I like this book because it's about cats. | Other characters in the story think Shay is popular and a good person. A good person doesn't charge friends for gifts. Shay charged her friends for friendship bracelets! Who does that to a friend? | There is controversy around U.S. citizens being allowed to own and carry a weapon. On the one hand . . . An opposing view is . . . My current thinking is . . . because . . . |
| **Elaboration** | Cats make good pets because they are warm and like to cuddle. | I can relate to not standing up to a person because something similar happened to me in second grade. A popular boy told me to do something that I didn't want to do. I went along with his idea and got in trouble. I knew better but I wanted him to like me. | I agree it should be more difficult to get a gun. More thorough background checks with a psych evaluation might help. There should be a limit to how many and the types of guns a person can have and a license renewal should be required every three to four years. What other requirements should be included before licenses are issued? |
| **Evaluation** | Cats are the best pets because . . . | I think the themes in these two books are similar. Both main characters in these books . . . I know, because . . . | After reading and hearing about the issues around the right to own and carry a gun, I think . . . because . . . |
| **Questioning** | Why do you like cats? | How is Ally in *Fish in a Tree* like Carley in *One for the Murphys?* | Why should rules governing hunting be more protective of the prey than rules governing concealed weapon carriers? |

continued →

| Form of Discourse | Primary | Intermediate | Secondary |
|---|---|---|---|
| **Disagreement** | All animals don't eat the same kind of food because . . . | I disagree with your opinion of the role Shay plays in the story. Most settings are about Ally, not Shay. She's not that important to the story. | I disagree that we should allow all people to have guns. In this article it states *(cites statistics)*. If we allow people to have guns, we should at least have stricter gun rules that include . . . |
| **Synthesis** | People like pets. My cat is like my snuggly blanket. I don't want to go anywhere without it. | We talked about why Shay was in the story and how Ally's confidence grew from the beginning to the end of the book. Ally's confidence develops in the story just like Carley grows more secure in *One for the Murphys*. I didn't know that you could actually sense someone's confidence growing without the author actually telling us. | Banning handguns in the United States may not stop mass shootings because in one article we learned that although banning guns in the United Kingdom has stopped school shootings, more people are killing each other today than when guns were legal. Yet, according to a newspaper article in Melbourne, Australians have experienced different results. The author stated that gun-related homicides dropped 59 percent between 1995 and 2006 after gun control took effect. Since gun control produces mixed results in these two countries, a better solution to reduce the number of mass shootings in the United States might then be to instill tighter restrictions *before* guns are issued. |

## Tackling the Toughest Skills

After observing students of all grade levels talk in small groups, we have noticed how difficult it is for students to consistently apply the strategies and skills taught in focus lessons. For example, if a focus lesson is about asking thought-provoking questions to keep the conversation going, students may be able to ask questions immediately following the initial instruction. However, unless they have several opportunities to practice asking these questions and receive feedback about them, the skill is not embedded in their future conversations. Therefore, we advocate for approaching a cluster of focus lessons around a specific form of discourse, one explicitly taught as a unit of study to build skills for students just as they might develop skills in basketball as presented in this chapter's opening paragraphs.

As we have mentioned before, all conversation skills are important to explicitly teach, model, have students practice, and provide effective feedback. Noteworthy, there are four skills that cause particular difficulty for students to apply during their discussions. These skills include:

1. Asking good, effective questions
2. Citing evidence when making a claim or stating an opinion

3. Disagreeing and offering different perspectives—especially opposing views—of a topic, idea, or concept
4. Synthesizing to integrate new insights and elements from text with your existing schema to develop a more profound understanding

Each skill is explained more in depth and applied in the lesson progression examples this chapter describes. We contend that unless students can independently apply these skills, they may not attain discussions complete with deep, rich academic discourse.

## Revisiting Feedback

In chapter 2 (page 15), we explained the benefits and use of effective feedback to promote and enhance healthy, robust discussions. Group oral feedback about a general observation, a common pattern, or a misconception can be helpful in advancing the understanding for all students. Individual feedback can range from a more formal and structured process, as used in student-teacher conferring sessions, to an informal sharing of a few words after we witness an individual student applying a learning target or working well on an individual goal. Feedback helps students decide how they are progressing toward meeting the learning targets and what they do next regardless of the discussion format (Brookhart, 2008).

Feedback is a critical element in learning progressions. When feedback is clear, concise, specific, and helpful, student learning explodes. It sets up students for success and ensures all students know what is needed to improve and progress to the next level. To that end, you must articulate and discuss what success looks and sounds like before students begin any activity, project, presentation, or discussion. We call these *look-fors*, and they align with the specific learning targets.

## Teaching Students Questioning Skills

It is important to develop students' questioning skills, both as they read and when they engage in dialogue. Questions about narrative text may focus on figuring out themes, symbols, motives, the author's purpose and technique, underlying meanings of the action within the story, character development, and word choice. Whereas, questions generated from reading nonfiction texts require thinking and pondering about interpretation, perspectives, identifying importance, persuading, recognizing bias, and inferring cause and effect. To demonstrate high levels of literacy, as called for in the CCSS, students must demonstrate that they can think deeply about, speak, and write in response to questions that address these areas.

While students read, they should write probing questions to gain deeper understanding. When students wait to construct questions until after reading, their initial thoughts, reactions, and wonderings that were provoked during reading often escape them. Questions generated *during the discussion* help clarify the speaker's points, deepen understanding of important concepts, and gain knowledge of other perspectives. Therefore, asking good questions must be taught, practiced, and applied in both contexts—while reading and in discussions—in order to reach deep discourse.

Students bring questions they wrote and pondered while reading to their small groups because, without this preparation, the type and level of questions are less rigorous than the ones they develop on the fly when they converse. Eventually, these on-the-fly questions also propel discussion forward and encourage other group members to keep digging to arrive at deeper understandings. Since good readers ask questions as they read, students practice authentic communication tasks while developing good reading habits. Video 6.1 "Grade 5: Questioning to Probe Deeper Thinking" demonstrates the power of fifth-grade students asking all types of questions to probe deeper thinking and learning from each other during a discussion about child labor.

## Feedback and Data Collection for Questioning

Take a look at figure 6.1 where the look-fors or indicators for questioning are delineated for teacher or student use. While observing students during class or discussion, you should collect evidence to share with individuals or groups. The feedback you provide at the end of the lesson sets up students for the next day's learning target and work—it is timely and specific, therefore giving students the opportunity to reflect and immediately apply their new learning to their next discussion.

| Indicator | Evidence |
|---|---|
| Asks questions that *clarify ideas of others* (What do you mean by . . .? How does that idea or example connect to . . .?) | |
| Generates questions to *identify reasons or evidence* a speaker provides to support particular points (How does that evidence connect or support your idea? What is a good example or a bad example of . . .? What evidence supports that idea?) | |
| Poses questions that *lead to deeper thinking* (Which is best . . .? How did they feel about . . .? How does this apply to . . .? What were some of the causes for . . .? What effect did . . . have on . . .?) | |
| Constructs questions that *seek other perspectives* (What are your thoughts about . . .? What other ideas should we consider to fully understand this topic?) | |
| Creates questions that *elicit good responses to expand understanding* about an idea or topic (How can we go deeper and explore this idea more fully? Can you provide an example to help us think about it in a different, unique, creative way? What evidence in the text will help us broaden our thinking?) | |

**Figure 6.1:** Data-collection guide for the use of questions.

*Visit* ***go.SolutionTree.com/instruction*** *for a free reproducible version of this figure.*

## Making Use of Data

In working with and observing teachers in several grade levels, we noted that many share a similar struggle: they don't know what to do with the student data they collected. The data collected serve two clear purposes—(1) supplying teachers with their next steps for instruction and (2) offering specific ways for students to improve their performance and learning. Furthermore, you can use the data-collection guide (figure 6.1) as you observe students in their discussions. The more specific data you can provide to students—as a class, group, and individually—the better students will perform while continuing to improve their communication skills.

We suggest using this data-collection guide while watching the video clips provided in this chapter to become more familiar with it prior to using it with students. Observation and record keeping are part of the application of learning for the lesson progressions throughout this chapter. Teachers, at all times, formally and informally make observations and monitor student progress and mastery of learning targets. They use these observations to provide feedback to students and guide future lessons. To facilitate and develop this process, we encourage you to practice gathering data during the application of learning section in each of lessons outlined in table 6.3 (page 112).

Table 6.3 is a lesson progression that provides ideas of increasing complexity to enhance students' questioning skills. Focus lessons 1 and 2 provide students with practice in developing questions using the Question-Answer Relationship (QAR) strategy (Raphael & Au, 2005). This strategy teaches students four levels of questioning used during reading and discussion: literal (right there), inferential (think and search), interpretive (author and me), and evaluative (on my own). If students already have had practice with developing questions, they need to know *when* questions can be used during conversations to propel them from good to great. Students can think about interjecting questions to:

- Clarify a vague comment
- Gain other perspectives about ideas or topics
- Bring other group members into the conversation
- Seek rationale for claims or interpretations
- Predict possible solutions or outcomes
- Make connections or organize information
- Solve problems
- Compare and contrast ideas or situations and look for commonalities
- Synthesize learning and articulate generalizations
- Assess or reflect on learning

**TABLE 6.3:** Lesson Progression for Questioning

<table>
<tr><td colspan="2">Lesson 1 learning target: I can develop at least two questions using the Question-Answer Relationship (QAR) strategy (Raphael & Au, 2005) including one author and me or on my own question as I read a piece of text. Note that students have been explicitly taught all four types of QAR questions: (1) right there, (2) think and search, (3) author and me, and (4) on my own.</td></tr>
<tr><td>Focus lesson and application of learning:<br>Mr. Ramos models the QAR strategy as he reads from a text. Prior to reading the text, he prepares a chart with the four types of questions (at right). While reading, he writes his questions about the text onto sentence strips, being sure to include one author and me or on my own question because they are good discussion questions.<br><br>After he finishes modeling his think-aloud, he classifies each question that he asked while reading right there, think and search, author and me, and on my own. Next, students read a text that they choose related to a topic of study. During their reading, they generate questions in the same manner Mr. Ramos did during the focus lesson. Later, they share examples of two questions they developed while reading the text with their partners and classify each type of question used.</td><td>Sentence stems or question prompts:<br><br>Right there—(The answer can be found in one place in the text.) Who (character) . . .? What (events, facts) . . .? Where and when (setting) . . .? How many . . .?<br><br>Think and search—(The answer is in the text; readers have to put together different parts of the text to find the answer.) What is the problem and how is it resolved? What role does (character's name) play in the story? What are the important events? What evidence in the text supports that argument?<br><br>Author and me—(The answer is not in the text; readers need to use their own ideas and experiences to answer the question.) What do you think will happen next? How would you describe the (mood, setting, plot) of the story and why is it important? What is the theme and how is it connected to the world beyond the story? How can we synthesize the information with what we know from other sources? How well does this author provide evidence for his or her view?<br><br>On my own—(The answer is not in the text; readers need to think about how the text and what they already know fit together.) What do we already know about this topic that can connect us to the story or text?</td></tr>
<tr><td colspan="2">Feedback: Mr. Ramos shares examples of questions using the QAR strategy he heard students use as they shared with their partners. In whole group, students share examples of questions they identify as they read the text and determine the types of questions they should practice using more.</td></tr>
<tr><td colspan="2">Lesson 2 learning target: I can generate and use at least two higher-level questions using the QAR strategy during discussion with my partner.</td></tr>
<tr><td>Focus lesson and application of learning:<br>Mr. Ramos revisits all four question types and explains that author and me and on my own questions are higher level because all students could have different answers to these types of questions during discussions, rather than one "right" answer.<br><br>During this lesson, Mr. Ramos provides a script of a short discussion for students to read and identify the type of questions used. Then, students read a different text or section of text on the content topic in this unit of study that began in lesson 1. After reading and jotting notes about the text, students create questions they will use during discussion with a partner that compare and contrast the information, actions, or problems about the text.</td><td>Sentence stems or question prompts:<br>• How is . . . similar to . . .?<br>• How can you determine . . .?<br>• What is your opinion of . . .?</td></tr>
<tr><td colspan="2">Feedback: Mr. Ramos shares examples of questions using the QAR strategy he heard during student discussions and asks students how they might follow up a question with probing questions to rethink or support the answer given. He informs his students that these questions require others to think at higher levels and justify answers. These answers are then taught and practiced in the next lesson.</td></tr>
</table>

<table>
<tr><td colspan="2">Lesson 3 learning target: I can ask for clarification when someone makes a vague comment or says something that I don't understand. Also, when I notice other group members are not participating in the discussion, I can ask a question that invites them to share their thoughts or ideas.</td></tr>
<tr><td>Focus lesson and application of learning:<br>Mr. Ramos shares some examples of questions that use the speaker's questions or answers as a bridge to further learning by asking the person to explain or clarify ("Can you tell us more?") or by asking the other students for their reactions ("What do others think about that idea?"). Then Mr. Ramos gives students a short piece of text with content from the unit of study for the students to practice the skill of asking follow-up, probing questions in their triad groups.</td><td>Sentence stems or question prompts:<br>• How do you know?<br>• Can someone else explain what (student's name) said but in a different way?<br>• Can you explain what you mean?<br>• What do you think about the idea that was just shared, (student's name)?<br>• (Student's name), do you agree with the ideas we talked about or do you have a different opinion?<br>• What can you add to this topic, (student's name)?</td></tr>
<tr><td colspan="2">Feedback: Mr. Ramos listens to pairs as they ask clarifying questions and use questions to invite members into the conversation, making notes of some questions he heard. After sharing specific examples of these questions with one to two groups, he shares common patterns noted across all groups with the whole class. The patterns he finds are that students asked clarifying questions to stimulate a response from the speaker, but they didn't extend the idea and further develop the concept. Instead, they jump to another thought or concept. He thinks students need to see video clips of the power of effective discussions where students make comparisons, build connections, and organize information to look for commonalities.</td></tr>
<tr><td colspan="2">Lesson 4 learning target: When other members of the group share ideas, I can dig deeper into these ideas by making comparisons and building connections to other ideas, my learning, or experiences in the world. Sometime before the discussion concludes, I can organize the information we talked about and highlight common themes or key ideas.</td></tr>
<tr><td>Focus lesson and application of learning:<br>Mr. Ramos shows a video clip of a discussion where students are making connections and building on ideas by comparing or contrasting the topic to other things they have either read about or talked about in other discussions. Mr. Ramos provides a video guide for things to watch for in the video. Each person in the group selects one thing to watch for and later will be responsible for providing vivid examples of what the students in the video said or did. One student notes the questions that were asked while another watches for connections made to other ideas, their learning, or real-world experiences. The third member of the group notes who is involved in the discussion and ways students share talking time (which helps to reinforce lesson 3). The fourth member of the group watches how students organize information to determine common themes or note key ideas. Students meet in small groups to discuss their observations. Then Mr. Ramos posts a chart that contains questions to make comparisons, build connections, and organize their thoughts to note key ideas. Next, students use the texts they have been reading to apply the skills they observed in the video.</td><td>Sentence stems or question prompts:<br>• What else do we know about that's similar to this idea?<br>• How does what we talked about connect with . . .?<br>• How does the information in this text compare to other texts on this topic we have read?<br>• How is . . . like . . .?<br>• What does the concept we are talking about have in common with the big idea of our discussion?<br>• What do all of the ideas we talked about today have in common?<br>• Let's organize our thoughts to develop some conclusions. What are the key ideas we talked about and what conclusions can we draw from them?</td></tr>
<tr><td colspan="2">Feedback: Mr. Ramos listens and takes notes as students talk about their observations from the video and their discussions about the texts their groups have been reading. He meets with groups to share specific examples of questions they asked during discussion and asks whether the questions gave them access to new information about the topic. For the benefit of all, students reconvene in whole group for Mr. Ramos, peers, or both to share two to three examples of connections or comparisons they made in their discussions. Then he shares an example of a group that he noted had organized their thoughts to highlight and reinforce their new learning.</td></tr>
</table>

continued →

<table>
<tr><td colspan="2">Lesson 5 learning target: I can ask at least two questions during discussion that stimulate connections, synthesize learning, and articulate generalizations across the multiple texts I have read on this topic as well as between what I have read and what I already know.</td></tr>
<tr><td>Focus lesson and application of learning:<br>Mr. Ramos shows a video clip of a discussion with the use of good questions. Students note qualities of questions that stimulate deep thought and discussion while Mr. Ramos writes them on an anchor chart. He asks students to listen specifically for questions that make connections, synthesize their learning, or articulate generalizations among ideas presented in text from multiple sources. Students post great discussion questions to a class chart with the title, Questions That Make Us Think. Next, Mr. Ramos either gives students a piece of text to read on the topic under study or students choose their own reading. Then, students meet in small groups to discuss the content, making connections or contrasting the ideas across the texts they have read on this topic, being sure to apply the use of questions to deepen understanding about the topic.</td><td>Sentence stems or question prompts:<br>• What are the key pieces of information we learned about from these texts?<br>• What have we discovered today and how will it help us?<br>• What conclusions can we draw and how has our thinking changed as a result of our discussion?<br>• What will we do differently now that we know more about this topic?</td></tr>
<tr><td colspan="2">Feedback: Mr. Ramos listens and provides feedback to small groups on one to two specific questions used in their discussions and asks them how the questions impacted their discussions. Additionally, he videotapes some group discussions in the class to share with the group, class, or both in later lessons.</td></tr>
<tr><td colspan="2">Lesson 6 learning target: I can analyze the types of responses our questions produce and make changes to two questions in order to generate a more thoughtful, significant discussion.</td></tr>
<tr><td>Focus lesson and application of learning:<br>Mr. Ramos shows a video clip of a discussion (either from students in the class or another). Students look for the types of responses their questions generate and note qualities of good responses to questions that stimulate deep thought and discussion. Meanwhile, Mr. Ramos writes them on an anchor chart. Students are encouraged to continue to add to the chart of great questions used in their discussions that they created during lesson 5, broadening the scope to have students think about the responses that great questions generate. Next, Mr. Ramos either gives students a piece of text to read on the topic under study, or they choose their own reading. Later, they have a small-group discussion incorporating their new learning.</td><td>Sentence stems or question prompts:<br>• What are the key pieces of information we learned about from this text?<br>• The author's message or point of view is . . .<br>• I think that the author makes or does not make a strong argument for . . . because . . .<br>• The information in (text 1) is similar and different than in (text 2) in a number of ways. (List at least three similarities and differences.)<br>• How does the information we learned impact me or the world?</td></tr>
<tr><td colspan="2">Feedback: Mr. Ramos displays the notes he took during discussion to record the different types of responses students make. He points out the strongest responses and deeper discussions developed from the higher-level questions group members' ask. Mr. Ramos asks students to reflect about how others respond to their comments during discussion and if those responses led to new thinking and learning. Responding to others remains a critical focus because they are what propel discussion.</td></tr>
</table>

After observing discussions from students of all grade levels, we believe students benefit from knowing *how* to craft a variety of questions and *when to use them* during discussion to elicit deeper understanding and new learning.

Because lesson progressions are a series of lessons designed to move students toward mastery of a particular learning goal, in this table (6.3, page 112) we move students incrementally along that continuum using focus lessons of increasing rigor and complexity. Even with the most carefully designed instruction, students may struggle or excel with the learning target. When this happens, consider developing an additional focus lesson that includes sentence stems or talking prompts to cultivate communication skills.

## Emphasizing a Certain Skill

Despite the fact that students need all the conversational skills to converse effectively in groups, you can have them work deliberately on one particular skill in order to improve it. For example, if students are working to enhance their questioning skills, it is often helpful to show a video of students asking a variety of questions during their discussions, as used in lessons 4 to 6 in the lesson progression table 6.3 outlines.

Videotaping your students during discussion may seem awkward for them at first; however, the video provides a visual for students to watch and rewatch as they hone in on a particular skill or learning target. Students quickly become used to this practice and find that videos are an excellent tool for their learning and progress toward solid student-led discussion behaviors and skills.

Teachers can also use videos as a formative assessment tool to determine their next steps for instruction or, during a focus lesson, to support the execution of a particular learning target, making it visual for students. Another benefit of video use for both students and teachers is analyzing their discussions to construct specific feedback for groups and individuals. When each group member looks for key points you want to highlight, and then the group discusses their findings together, you reinforce the importance of each member's contributions while providing a visual model of a conversation that effectively uses questioning.

Students need to be able to analyze the use of good questioning skills. As students talk about the video, they should determine what is (or is not) effective as well as what is needed to make effective questioning part of the conversation. Sometimes students generate a checklist in their notebooks or an anchor chart to post on the wall of good questioning techniques to help them increase their proficiency with this skill. This type of scaffolding gives students the support they need as they work toward conversing without checklists, prompts, or anchor charts.

Often, *we* want to generate the questions that get conversations started for students, or stop them as they engage in their conversations to ask questions that spur their thinking. When you assist your own students in these ways, you need to remember that the goal is to have *them* generate their own questions and prompts, similar to or better than the ones we might pose. The questions must reside with the students to develop their thinking and questioning abilities. You need to help them develop the capability to ask tough and meaningful questions. Author and professor of education Nancy Lee Cecil (1995) states:

> Students attain significantly higher levels of thinking when they are encouraged to develop skills in generating critical and creative questions and when they are provided opportunities for dialogue with classmates about the questions posed and conclusions derived from information they encounter. (p. 36)

Students often come up with better, more thought-provoking questions than we could have ever imagined when they're responsible for asking and answering questions!

## Citing Textual Evidence

Citing textual evidence substantiates an idea or opinion about a topic, problem, or question and supports that claim with enough evidence and reasoning to be convincing. The speaker's task in discussions is similar to that of a lawyer who must argue a position before a jury. As a result, students learn that strong text evidence is an invaluable tool when persuading others that their claims, ideas, or theories are plausible.

To achieve this goal during discussion, students must be well organized, clear, and convincing in presenting their claims and supporting evidence. The objective is to influence. Therefore, students need to learn to explain and prove the main idea, from introduction to conclusion, from one substantiating point to the next, in a manner that allows others to understand the claim clearly and permits the rest of the group little reason to doubt it.

When students are able to present their claims persuasively in their small-group discussions, they are much more apt to produce effective, persuasive, and powerful writing. In video 6.2 "Grade 9: Citing Textual Evidence During Discussion," a group of ninth-grade students cites textual evidence as the group alludes to specific examples to support its ideas during small-group discussion. Citing text evidence begins long before ninth grade and continues in educational standards through graduation.

We plan the scaffolding students will need by thinking about where students may begin and what we want them to learn. For the use of textual evidence in seventh grade, the Common Core Reading standards require students to cite several pieces of textual evidence to support an analysis of what the text says explicitly as well as inferences drawn from the text (NGA & CCSSO, 2010a). When planning, it is important to look at the Reading standards in grades 6 and 8 as well. The differences in these standards are that sixth-grade students just need to cite textual evidence while eighth-grade students need to find textual evidence that *strongly* supports a claim or position, which means they need to judge the value of their proof. The videos 6.3 and 6.4 "Grades 4–5: Focus Lesson for Evaluating Evidence" and "Grades 4–5: Small Group

With Teacher" consist of a teacher delivering a focus lesson that models how students can evaluate evidence to strengthen an argument and its application during small-group discussion.

In the Speaking and Listening CCSS, sixth-grade students delineate a speaker's argument, distinguishing claims that are supported by reasons and evidence from claims that are not (NGA & CCSSO, 2010a). The learning progression for this task notches up in seventh grade to have students judge the sufficiency of the evidence. Eighth grade extends this further by requiring students to determine when *irrelevant* evidence is introduced (NGA & CCSSO, 2010a). The CCSS for Writing align with these skills and applications. At the close of the lesson in video 6.5 "Grades 4–5: Feedback and Closure," you'll see how students merge new learning and critical-thinking skills following a discussion where text evidence was evaluated by students and used for application to bigger real-world ideas.

With these goals in mind, you should begin thinking about the many ways you will support your students. How will you explicitly teach students to cite evidence that credibly supports their claims? What do they need to know when they cite evidence in writing and how does that compare to how they cite evidence when they speak? For example, seventh-grade students might know how to identify text evidence, but they might not know how to use it when they talk in their small groups or later in their writing.

After you assess your students' familiarity with locating text evidence to support their claims, the focus lessons in table 6.4 (page 118) might be helpful when thinking about the lesson progression. This learning progression relates to the standard, "Cite textual evidence to support analysis of what the text says explicitly as well as inferences drawn from the text" (RL.6.1; NGA & CCSS, 2010a), but you can easily apply it to other CCSS, such as asking questions, making inferences, or analyzing text.

Just as the table provides one learning progression example, the videos linked to this chapter also provide an example of a learning progression. They do not link directly to the example in the table, but rather showcase another Common Core standard.

**TABLE 6.4:** Lesson Progression for Citing Textual Evidence

**Lesson 1 learning target:** I can identify and share at least three pieces of text to support the big content ideas while reading.

**Focus lesson and application of learning:**
Ms. Jackson distributes a short piece of text to use with this lesson. Before students read the article, she creates an anchor chart with three headings written across the top: (1) question, (2) response, and (3) text evidence. First, she models one example of a think and search or interpretative question, response, and the evidence found in the text. Next, students work with partners to generate another question and complete the other two columns. Then, students practice to complete two more examples using this text. For follow-up application, Ms. Jackson provides another related article for students to read, develop interpretative questions, find evidence, and write their responses into their readers' notebooks using a similar chart as modeled.

**Sentence stems or question prompts:**

- In this article, I think the author is letting us know . . . because (paraphrase textual evidence).
- I think the big idea of this article is . . . because (provide textual evidence).
- The most compelling reason for . . . is (opinion or claim) because in this article it states . . .

**Example:**

| Questions | Response | Text Evidence |
|---|---|---|
| Using information from the article, what can you conclude about the number of books Jose read before he pledged to read forty books in fifth grade? | He read fewer books than most other fifth-grade students. | Jose only read one book last year and none in third grade. According to the graph, most fourth-grade students read more than ten books and third-grade students read more than twenty. |
| What is one effect that *not reading* might have on Jose's success in school? | Jose might fail a test because he didn't read the assignment. | Students sometimes don't have good reading habits. Therefore, the slightest distractions prevent them from completing their reading assignments. |

**Feedback:** Ms. Jackson shares that students were successful when citing multiple pieces of text evidence to support the big ideas while reading. She noticed most students copying the exact sentence that was written in the article when recording their evidence onto the chart and knows that next steps will include modeling and teaching students how to pull quotes, reference an author, and paraphrase text evidence into their own words. Reflecting on discussion, Ms. Jackson highlights students' use of open-ended questions and shares that these types of questions are strong because they allow for others' answers to be different from their own. In the next lesson, students will cite evidence in multiple ways to answer questions and support responses during discussion.

| **Lesson 2 learning target:** I can capture evidence in three different ways *while* reading in order to illustrate my points—making a reference to the author or the text, paraphrasing the author by telling about the ideas or story in my own words, and directly quoting from the text. | |
|---|---|
| **Focus lesson and application of learning:**<br>Ms. Jackson uses a short nonfiction text to model making a reference to the author or the text, paraphrasing the author by telling about the ideas in her own words, and directly quoting from the text. Students use the say something strategy while reading, with a specific focus on citing textual evidence. Students are given a short nonfiction text specific to the content being studied to read and discuss with a partner.<br>Before reading, students predict the issue or idea being presented in the text and then read to find evidence to support or cause them to alter their predictions. As students begin reading, they should pause after each paragraph or section of text to discuss and present evidence in support of or rebutting their prediction, or cite specific evidence by referencing the author, paraphrasing, or directly quoting the text that challenges their partner's prediction or earlier response. | **Sentence stems or question prompts:**<br>• I think when (cite author's name) wrote, (select a word or phrase from the text) it meant . . .<br>• The event in (cite book) where the author describes (paraphrase portion of text) impacts . . .<br>• What do you think the author means by (present quote from text)?<br>• Why do you think the author wrote (quote)?<br>• What did it mean when (paraphrase)? |
| **Feedback:** Ms. Jackson heard several students directly quoting and referring to the text to support their thinking about the topic. Her feedback for students references specific examples she recorded while observing discussion groups. Ms. Jackson adds for students that these examples provide credible evidence to establish or back up an argument. Paraphrasing the author in their own words during discussion continues to be an area of growth and will be the sole focus during her next lesson. | |
| **Lesson 3 learning target:** I can identify and use the following steps of citing evidence by stating an idea, paraphrasing the text that led to that idea, and explaining the evidence when talking with my partner. | |
| **Focus lesson and application of learning:**<br>Ms. Jackson creates a chart during her modeling with three headings: (1) stating an idea, (2) paraphrasing the text, and (3) explaining the evidence to help students cite evidence from text. She articulates and records ideas that surface as she thinks aloud while reading. After recording each idea, she paraphrases the specific quote or statement from the text that prompted or supported her thinking. Next, she provides support for students by generating sentence stems or talk prompts and writing them on an anchor chart for their later reference during discussion. Lastly, she releases students to discuss their ideas, paraphrase citations, and explain to partners the use of evidence. | **Sentence stems or question prompts:**<br>• I think . . . (my idea) is supported by . . . which means . . .<br>• The author's main point is . . . The evidence in the text that supports this claim is (paraphrase text evidence). To me this means . . .<br>• I think one point in this article is . . . because the text states (paraphrase the text) which means . . .<br>• In this section, the author states that (share main idea). Other points in this text that support this idea are . . . I interpret this to mean . . .<br>• The author explains (paraphrase the text)<br>• This illustrates (explain the evidence) which causes me to believe . . .<br>• This reveals (explain the evidence). To me this means . . . |
| **Feedback:** Ms. Jackson informs the whole group that she heard several of the sentence stems used during conversation and provides specific examples. Next, she asks, "How can we respond to others using new evidence during discussion in an efficient manner? How could you use text evidence to challenge someone else's idea?" Students know they will receive guidance and support as they learn more about this next step in an upcoming lesson. | |

continued →

<table>
<tr><td colspan="2">Lesson 4 learning target: I can locate and cite new textual evidence during discussion to support or extend an idea, evidence, or claim others present.</td></tr>
<tr><td>Focus lesson and application of learning:<br>Ms. Jackson projects a script of a discussion to show how students utilize textual evidence during discussion to support or extend other group members' ideas. She asks four students to read the script while others listen for these extensions. After this demonstration and follow-up discussion, each student is assigned one subtopic or issue presented in the text to become an "expert" for discussion.<br><br>During discussion, each student listens for opportunities to share specific textual evidence (statements, direct quotes, or paraphrasing) to support or challenge the ideas group members present. This sharing may be preceded or followed up with probing questions to keep the discussion on point, avoid slowing conversation in real time, propel further discussion, and ultimately, deepen student understanding.</td><td>Sentence stems or question prompts:<br>• I can add to (student's name)'s point. In this article it states that (paraphrase), so I think...<br>• I agree with (student's name)'s point about . . . and I'd like to add . . . because . . .<br>• After listening to you share, I'd like to expand on your thinking about . . . because . . .<br>• In the first paragraph, it states... which presents a similar view from the one you just shared. I think . . .</td></tr>
<tr><td colspan="2">Feedback: Ms. Jackson provides specific feedback of how the discussion was extended by additional comments and evidence. Then, she informs them that she only heard evidence in support of a position. She notes that no positions, ideas, or examples were challenged while she observed. Therefore, this area will be the next lesson's focus.</td></tr>
<tr><td colspan="2">Lesson 5 learning target: I can challenge at least one other person's ideas based on textual evidence or inferences drawn from textual evidence. (Note: Since this is a difficult concept for students to apply and use regularly in their discussions, the skill is introduced here but should be explored more deeply as presented in the Disagreeing section on page 122.)</td></tr>
<tr><td>Focus lesson and application of learning:<br>Ms. Jackson reads aloud a picture book about a controversial or difficult period in history. For this lesson, Ms. Jackson uses The Other Side (Woodson, 2001), a picture book depicting the story of two young girls challenging the racial divide between African Americans and whites, but any other picture book could be used. Next, she reads a current article that presents at least one of the same issues or themes as the read-aloud. She demonstrates comparing and contrasting the texts using the skills learned in lessons 1–4 to support her claims with textual evidence. Then she shows a video clip of a discussion where students:<br>• Use specific textual evidence to support or challenge ideas, reasoning, other evidence, or all of the above<br>• Pose questions from ideas and opinions that surface from information and comments others shared during discussion<br>• Restate someone's comment and expand on the idea by using additional textual evidence<br>• Make a contribution that is a continuation of a current exchange<br><br>These items serve as the look-for indicators for students to use as they watch the video. After viewing the video, students are released to practice applying these skills in their small-group discussions.</td><td>Sentence stems or question prompts:<br>• I disagree with (thought, idea, or evidence) because . . . So, I believe . . .<br>• The point you made is similar to my idea in that . . . However, I think we also need to consider . . . because . . .<br>• How does that evidence relate to this point?<br>• How is the example you provided from the text relevant to our topic?<br>• What example or evidence from the text can you provide for the point you are trying to make?<br>• On what evidence did you base your opinion?<br>• In this text it said . . .<br>• I'd like to expand on (student's name)'s idea that . . . My view is . . . because . . .</td></tr>
</table>

**Feedback:** Ms. Jackson commends students on their ability to restate the speaker's ideas and information. She adds that the connections made during discussion were spot on. Moving forward, she reinforces the importance of discussion groups needing to be a safe place where it is okay for all students to disagree respectfully with another's idea or opinion. Ms. Jackson advises students to be confident when challenging another group member and shares that making direct statements supported with text evidence during discussion will assist them in this endeavor.

## Finding Look-Fors in Video Clips

As we explained earlier, there are advantages to showing video clips of students engaged in discussions where members are citing textual evidence. It helps to have students generate some of the look-for indicators that would be present if they applied the skill effectively. Then, each group member assumes responsibility for looking for a couple of indicators in the video discussion. In video 6.6 "Grade 5: Negotiating the Main Idea," students use textual evidence to help determine the main idea of nonfiction text.

Figure 6.2 offers an example of indicators or look-fors you might use as students view a corresponding video.

| Indicator | Evidence in Video |
|---|---|
| Makes reference to a title, author, or both | |
| Paraphrases the author by telling about ideas in own words | |
| Uses direct quotes relevant to topic | |
| Selects details from text and makes inferences based on evidence in text and prior knowledge | |
| Presents claims and supporting evidence with pertinent descriptions, facts, and details to emphasize main idea or topic | |
| Locates and cites evidence when responding to the challenges others pose, emphasizing salient points in a focused, coherent manner | |
| Challenges others' ideas based on textual evidence or inferences drawn from text | |

*Visit* ***go.SolutionTree.com/instruction*** *for a free reproducible version of this figure.*

**Figure 6.2:** Video guide for citing textual evidence during a discussion.

Discussions give students an authentic reason to use and explain textual and interpretative evidence. But without modeling, practice with support, and proper feedback, students will struggle with the challenge of meaningfully supporting their claims. As with all CCSS, teaching students to substantiate their responses with verification cannot be a one-and-done lesson. You should provide ample opportunities for students to learn and practice using evidence in their oral discussions, as well as written assignments, while continuing to emphasize this practice until students can do it habitually, without support or reminders.

## Disagreeing

In the midst of any conversation there are bound to be moments when members have heard statements or opinions that conflict with their beliefs or thinking about a subject. In any group discussion, students may disagree passionately, but this is healthy, normal behavior. Actually, teaching students how to listen to others' ideas and respect their points of view is a fundamental Speaking and Listening standard that appears in the CCSS as early as first grade and progresses there forward. In third grade, students are supposed to be taught and learn how to cooperate and compromise. Sixth-grade students need to cooperate, mediate, and problem solve to make decisions; and by eighth grade, they need to learn how to build consensus.

Argument is one important writing genre the CCSS stress. Beginning in first grade, students must supply reasons for their beliefs when they write opinion pieces. The requirements of writing argumentation are quite sophisticated for high school students. Besides using evidence in their written arguments, they must also establish the relationships and their value among claims, counterclaims, reasons, and evidence.

To argue or disagree in an academic context is to state an opinion through the process of reasoning and persuasion, supported by rational evidence. Many learners interpret the term *argument* to mean a fight between people where one tries to dominate the other in order to win. Without instruction, students may not know how to move the discussion beyond personal insults that characterize a fight.

Academic arguments or disagreements aim to explore a question, a proposition, or an area of knowledge, and achieve reasoned mutual understanding. It is not important who wins—what matters most is the quality of the argument and the understanding that results. When students disagree in their discussions, we believe they develop new ideas, advance and clarify their knowledge, and learn to think critically. Furthermore, students develop and utilize communication skills during conflicts because they must anticipate any questions or concerns others may have and think carefully about how to respond. Disagreements require negotiation skills where the best possible outcome is a resolution that benefits all parties.

Disagreement commands that students combine their knowledge of content, active reading strategies, and speaking and listening skills. When students bring up opposing views during discussion and support them with evidence, others think, reflect, find new evidence, and respond to those challenges. Inevitably, as students dialogue back and forth, asking probing questions and citing new evidence to combat others' arguments, an increased focus on the topic leads to consideration of different perspectives and new understanding. Disagreement compels students to go deeper during discussion.

Some of the most educational conversations involve the arguing and negotiating of differing ideas. This type of talk includes several highly valued skills. These skills include the ability to productively critique ideas, consider reinforced points, evaluate the value of claims, and make collaborative decisions (Mercer, 1995).

Many ideas and decisions in life are not right or wrong. They are abstract, complex, evolving, and made up of words that convey different interpretations. *Negotiation* means to discuss a matter with intent to reach agreement. As students negotiate meaning through discussion they form a mutual understanding by conceding some points and adding others from their partners. The object is not to win, but to understand and build stronger ideas. Table 6.5 provides a sample lesson progression to help students develop and enhance these important skills.

**TABLE 6.5:** Lesson Progression for Teaching About Disagreement

<table>
<tr><td colspan="2">Lesson 1 learning target: I can read and analyze text to anticipate opposing viewpoints and prepare a thoughtful, supported response with evidence to support it.</td></tr>
<tr><td>Focus lesson and application of learning:<br>Mr. Pham distributes an article about a current controversial topic: cell phones in schools. He introduces the issue and, using a graphic organizer, briefly models how to collect supporting evidence about both sides of the controversy. He chooses a side to defend and asks students what those who disagree with him might bring up as an argument during discussion. Following this, he goes back to his graphic organizer and finds evidence to rebut the opposing view and uses that information to prepare a thoughtful counterargument. Students then read a new article about a controversial topic and choose one side to defend. While reading, they complete the same process modeled and are then placed into small groups where they use text evidence to support their opinions and challenge others' arguments.</td><td>Sentence stems or question prompts:<br>• One view on the topic of . . . is . . . Another view is . . . The most compelling reasons in support of the each view are . . .<br>• Two conflicting views are: (1) . . . and (2) . . . The evidence in support of the first view is . . . and the evidence in support of the second view is . . .</td></tr>
<tr><td colspan="2">Feedback: Mr. Pham listens as partners share the issues and supporting evidence they found in the text. After providing whole-group feedback using specific examples he captured, he collects their work to use for the next lesson.</td></tr>
<tr><td colspan="2">Lesson 2 learning target: I can respectfully challenge an idea I don't agree with during discussion and respond appropriately when my idea, claim, or evidence is challenged.</td></tr>
<tr><td>Focus lesson and application of learning:<br>Mr. Pham uses examples from students' lesson 1 work to share ideas that might not have aligned. Then he models how he might introduce an opposing view, using some sentence stems or talking prompts. Next, he points out how this example demonstrates how to respectfully challenge an idea, claim, or evidence rather than an individual. He provides one to two examples of challenging another person disrespectfully. Finally, students are given a choice of three to four articles to read that contain opposing views, then discuss and practice with a partner a conversation that contains disagreement.</td><td>Sentence stems or question prompts:<br>• I don't agree with the idea about . . . I think . . .<br>• I'm confused about . . . Would you explain with more detail and examples?<br>• One thing I'd like to challenge is . . . because . . .<br>• I can see why you might believe . . ., but have you thought about . . . ?</td></tr>
<tr><td colspan="2">Feedback: After Mr. Pham listens and takes notes from several pairs, he realizes that students make a point, disagree with supporting evidence, and then move on to the next point without further elaboration. He shares with the whole group some specific examples of word choices that were used when students disagreed with a claim, notes that he heard students disagree with ideas, but did not hear anyone support his or her disagreement with supporting evidence. Lastly, he shares his observation about the need for further elaboration supporting or challenging the opposing view. He assigns additional reading on the topic as homework for the next lesson's discussion.</td></tr>
</table>

continued →

<table>
<tr><td colspan="2">Lesson 3 learning target: I can take a side of a point or issue brought up and offer supporting testimony to deepen my understanding of a topic, idea, or perspective.</td></tr>
<tr><td>Focus lesson and application of learning:<br>Mr. Pham shows a video clip of students who make a point and offer supporting evidence to that claim. In this video clip, ideas are challenged or supported and other members of the group elaborate on the idea by taking a side contributing further evidence or reasons to dig deep into the topic. Students use a video viewing guide to take notes of specific examples to later talk about in their groups. Mr. Pham explains that they will be talking about how the discussion flowed among the group and asks them to specifically look for questions, ideas, or examples used to elaborate on the topic. After the viewing, students meet in their small groups to discuss look-fors. Equipped with a good example, students discuss the additional reading assigned from the previous day to deliberate new ideas on this evolving topic.</td><td>Sentence stems or question prompts:<br>• I can see your point and I'd like to add . . .<br>• That's a good point, and some evidence I found to further support that view is . . .<br>• I see what you're getting at or where you're coming from, but I think. . . because . . .<br>• I see what you mean; however I think (makes a point) is relevant to consider because . . .</td></tr>
<tr><td colspan="2">Feedback: Mr. Pham records and shares many examples of students taking a side and supporting it with evidence. Then he asks students what questions they might ask to gain a better understanding of a view other than their own. These questions can be used as stems for the next lesson.</td></tr>
<tr><td colspan="2">Lesson 4 learning target: I can generate and ask questions to gain understanding of opposing views.</td></tr>
<tr><td>Focus lesson and application of learning:<br>Mr. Pham observed and talked to a particularly skillful group the previous day about using it to model its questions during discussion in a fishbowl strategy for the rest of the class. Mr. Pham specifically asks members to include the sentence stems generated and posted on an anchor chart for their viewing. As the inner circle engages in a discussion, the rest of the class takes notes on look-for items. After a whole-group discussion highlighting the times when questions helped to gain a better understanding of opposing views, students reconvene in small groups to discuss the next reading or topic, knowing that their teacher will be watching for their application of this new skill and providing them with feedback.</td><td>Sentence stems or question prompts:<br>• What's your concern about . . .?<br>• What's bothering you about this current position?<br>• What has to occur for you to comfortably support this view?<br>• Are you comfortable with any aspect of this perspective?</td></tr>
<tr><td colspan="2">Feedback: Mr. Pham captures specific examples to share with one to two small groups, but observes all groups to note patterns across the whole class. He shares these patterns, highlighting that most groups asked good questions to understand different views. Then he explains that the opposing views were brought up, discussed, and the conversations ended without trying to determine which view was most logical. Students know this will be the focus of the next lesson to help improve their skills.</td></tr>
</table>

<table>
<tr><td colspan="2">Lesson 5 learning target: I can negotiate value and importance of ideas, evidence, or examples and use logical reasoning to suggest a solution.</td></tr>
<tr><td>Focus lesson and application of learning: Now that students have applied all the skills in lessons 1–4, they are ready to mediate and problem solve to make decisions on the best solution to opposing views on ideas and evidence. Mr. Pham shows a video clip featuring this element of the discussion. Again, students are asked to look for specific items in the video (see figure 6.3, page 126) which they later talk about, either in small groups or as a whole class. Then students practice this skill with a new reading assignment on the ongoing topic or a new one that contains discussion-worthy ideas to generate opposing views.</td><td>Sentence stems or question prompts:<br>• It seems we have different points of view. I think the issues are . . . Do we all agree on these issues?<br>• Is it possible to . . . and . . . at the same time?<br>• I believe that view might be missing . . . It's needed because . . .<br>• Can we agree that . . .?<br>• All opinions are valued. Is there a different alternative that we can all agree on to reach a solution?<br>• Of all the ideas we discussed, the one that included the most logical reasoning supported with credible evidence was . . . because . . . How do you feel about this conclusion?</td></tr>
<tr><td colspan="2">Feedback: Mr. Pham listens for application of the new skills, notes specific examples, and shares them with the whole group. In order to make decisions about the best solution, which contains opposing views, some members of the group may need to change their position on the issue. He mentions that he heard statements like, "After hearing other perspectives, I've changed my thinking. I now think . . ." and "I used to think . . . but now I think . . . based on . . ." and "The compelling points that (student's name) made helped me to think differently. My new view is . . ." As Mr. Pham provides these examples he adds these sentence stems to chart paper and posts them for students to see and use in their future discussions.</td></tr>
</table>

A helpful practice when engaging in disagreement is to evaluate student understanding before and after discussion to determine what new learning or understandings were gained as a result of the discussion. If students didn't learn anything new, or experience having their own ideas challenged, exploring and examining the purpose and effectiveness of their questions becomes pertinent.

Sometimes students do not need every lesson provided in the lesson progression example. They may be particularly skillful and can readily apply the task with little direction and support. The lesson progression offers an alternative, one where the emphasis is on providing students with the conditions that align with the CCSS. There are some students who are able to argue meaningfully and respectfully while there are many who cannot. Students will get better at presenting their views when they have time, instruction, practice, and coaching on how to improve. It is critical that students know how to form logical arguments in presenting their opinions and how to challenge opposing views respectfully. Sometimes, students attack individuals or make unwarranted generalizations like "That idea is stupid," which shuts down the discussion and leaves the respondent feeling attacked. When it is done well, by listening attentively, showing empathy, and understanding rather than attacking different perspectives, the conversation flows and all members feel valued and respected.

Learning how to argue rationally isn't magic. For most students, good instruction makes the difference. Good instruction involves modeling—either by us, by students, or through the use of video—with supported practice, and is tailored to the students' needs based on ongoing assessment. These lesson progressions, along with the Disagreement Video Viewing Guide (figure 6.3), should provide you with the guidance needed for you to demonstrate this development.

| Indicators | Evidence in video |
|---|---|
| Respectfully challenges others' ideas | |
| Responds appropriately to challenges of own ideas | |
| Takes a side of a point or issue brought up and offers supporting testimony to deepen understanding of perspective | |
| Seeks agreement of ideas that are challenged | |
| Suggests a solution to two opposing views | |
| Asks questions to gain understanding of opposing views | |
| Modifies meaning in response to another view on same issue (negotiation) | |
| Supports claim with evidence and logical reasoning | |
| Changes mind by the logic of another member's argument | |
| Negotiates value and importance of ideas, evidence, or examples and uses logical reasoning to suggest a solution | |

**Figure 6.3** Disagreement video viewing guide.

*Visit **go.SolutionTree.com/instruction** for a free reproducible version of this figure.*

Disagreement can be difficult and some students as well as adults find it uncomfortable. But, with proper instruction, practice, and lots of feedback, you can equip your students with skills that they will use often in their lifetime.

# Synthesizing

The final skill we cover in this chapter is synthesizing. Synthesizing is complex because it interweaves prior knowledge with new perspectives, insights, and thinking to create something different—a realization, new meaning, or perhaps an aha idea. Synthesis organizes our thinking and connects what we already know to the learning taking place.

Synthesizing is a matter of pulling various sources together into some kind of harmony. It is the ability to combine, clearly and coherently, the ideas from more than one source with our own. It begins by pulling together the pieces of what we are learning at points during the journey of reading a text or experiencing some type of other media.

The CCSS for third grade require students to explain ideas and understanding in light of discussion. Then in fifth grade, students need to be able to draw conclusions in light of information and knowledge gained from discussions. Eighth-grade students need to acknowledge new information, qualify or justify their view, and make decisions or build consensus as appropriate. High school students synthesize comments, claims, and evidence made on all sides of an issue, resolve contradictions when possible, and determine what additional information is required to deepen the investigation or complete the task. In other words, we explicitly teach synthesizing in early elementary education and then help students build the rigor and complexity of their thinking throughout their education.

Synthesizing is largely a thinking process, one that may develop in many ways, particularly when students have opportunities to interact through discussions and writing. How do we synthesize? To better understand this concept, consider the example of a new school year.

As teachers, we are energized to tackle a new year using our past experiences in order to build relationships with students, plan lessons, confront challenges, and set goals aimed toward all students reaching their highest potential. Inevitably, as the school year progresses and we get to know our students as individuals, academically, and socially, the pacing of lessons and unit designs we had previously planned are modified to best meet all learners' needs. Our approach changes as the year progresses—once we think differently, we plan and instruct differently.

Our thinking changes as we read, learn about, and discuss a topic. What we once thought or believed to be true becomes history—this is *synthesis*: the process of fusing our old thinking with multiple sources of information and ideas to percolate and create something new.

So, when does synthesis occur during a discussion and what does it look like? Synthesis sometimes occurs during discussion to pull ideas together, but should always happen at the end. "How you close a discussion can determine what students will 'take with them' from the exercise" (Kachorek, 2009).

As each person shares his or her thinking, evidence, key information, and opinions while discussing a text or topic, the original ideas and perspectives are no longer held. Thinking evolves as aha moments evolve throughout the discussion. This synthesis process includes: jotting ideas that come to mind, taking notes on important points, expanding on or challenging statements others make, making decisions, summarizing the key discussion themes, and discovering novel ways to apply innovative learning. As the conversation comes to a close, each group member sees the concepts, ideas, or topic in a new way.

The fourth- through ninth-grades examples showcased in videos 6.7 and 6.8 "Grades 4–6: Synthesizing Using Multiple Texts" and "Grade 9: Synthesis With Profound Insights and Connections" reveal how powerful student-led discussions are when students synthesize information from multiple texts to determine big ideas and acquire new and different perspectives.

Table 6.6 offers a sample lesson progression showing how you may help students expand on their skills to synthesize more effectively.

As students view visual messages from video, they need to use a range of viewing skills and strategies to make sense of the visual images, and accompanying oral and print language. They need to derive meaning from it and respond personally, critically, and creatively.

The International Literacy Association (ILA) and National Council of Teachers of English (NCTE) agree that being literate means being active, critical, and creative users not only of print and spoken language but also of the visual language of film and television, commercial and political advertising, photography, and more (ILA, n.d.; NCTE, n.d.). Therefore, viewing videos of students as they engage in discussions not only helps them understand the next steps in their skill development but also provides them practice with being critical users of the visual language in video.

Capturing and maintaining student interest can be the toughest part of teaching. By presenting these short two- to six-minute video clips that illustrate the skills you are trying to teach, students maintain interest because they know they will be asked to apply the technique presented in the video in their next discussion. In these kinds of instances, showing a video clip at the right time can drive inquiry that makes otherwise abstract learning concepts much more meaningful. Figure 6.4 provides a guide to view students as they synthesize.

| Indicator | Evidence in Video |
|---|---|
| Makes note of important points brought up during discussion | |
| Discards ideas or points that weren't helpful | |
| Uses information from a variety of sources | |
| Organizes ideas in a meaningful, purposeful way | |
| Identifies and challenges points others make that aren't related to the focus of the conversation | |
| Remembers, highlights, and identifies key points of the discussion and summarizes these important parts | |
| Analyzes ideas and concepts to create something new | |
| Draws conclusions and makes generalizations to apply learning in a novel way | |

**Figure 6.4:** Video viewing guide for synthesis.

*Visit* ***go.SolutionTree.com/instruction*** *for a free reproducible version of this figure.*

By teaching students to explicitly look for related words, concepts, and ideas in the text, and using them to construct a main idea or summary statement, along with an aha or revelation, we provide tools for students to understand and apply this complex, important skill of synthesis.

**TABLE 6.6:** Synthesis Lesson Progression

<table>
<tr><td colspan="2">Lesson 1 learning target: I can think and jot notes while reading or during discussion to determine what is important as opposed to what is interesting about the topic.</td></tr>
<tr><td>Focus lesson and application of learning: Ms. Whitefeather uses the think-aloud strategy while previewing an article with students. She notices the title, subtitles, photos, captions, and other text features and records important information learned about the topic. She then reads the article.<br><br>During the entire think-aloud she stops at the end of each paragraph or section, jots a note, and shares a key point written by the author. Each section is summarized into one statement that someone who has never heard about this topic would need to know. This modeling places the emphasis on what is important rather than what is interesting. While thinking aloud, she might say, "Whoa! That is unbelievable to me," and specifically calls out that, while interesting, the particular piece of information isn't a key idea.<br><br>At the end of the think-aloud, Ms. Whitefeather reads the important ideas recorded during the think-aloud and writes a sentence or two illustrating her new thinking or perspective about the topic. By extending a summary of thoughts using multiple sources to include new thinking, she models the synthesis process. Students then choose an article to read with a partner or complete individually as they stop, jot while reading, and synthesize their key ideas recorded at the end.</td><td>Sentence stems or question prompts:<br>• I think this is mainly about . . .<br>• The most important idea is . . .<br>• The important ideas from the articles that I heard you talk about were . . .</td></tr>
<tr><td colspan="2">Feedback: Ms. Whitefeather provides specific examples of how students discussed important ideas and concepts as opposed to interesting facts that aren't relevant or key ideas about the topic. Then, she asks students to talk in small groups about how their thinking might change as they gain new knowledge. Next, she informs them they will continue to practice and focus on the changes in their thinking during the next lesson.</td></tr>
<tr><td colspan="2">Lesson 2 learning target: I can use the Facts, Questions, Response (FQR) strategy while reading or during discussion to monitor and illustrate the change in my thinking.</td></tr>
<tr><td>Focus lesson and application of learning: Ms. Whitefeather selects an article about a new or controversial topic to illustrate the FQR strategy. She constructs a three-column table with the headings: (1) facts, (2) questions, and (3) response. Through modeling, she demonstrates how she stops to record important facts, generates questions she is wondering about, and documents her thinking while reading. Then after reading another short selection, she highlights those spots where her thinking shifted or changed and then writes a statement or describes in a few sentences how she would explain that topic to someone who knows nothing about it. After providing a short guided practice with the next portion of the text for students to practice, she releases them to practice reading a new article (or finish that one if not complete) and later shares their changes in thinking highlighted from their FQR.<br><br><table><tr><th>Facts</th><th>Questions</th><th>Response</th></tr><tr><td></td><td></td><td></td></tr></table></td><td>Sentence stems or question prompts:<br>• Something I learned was . . . This idea or concept made me wonder, ". . .?" Now I think . . .<br>• I wonder how . . .<br>• I realized that . . .<br>• When I hear you say that I am wondering . . .<br>• I used to think . . . but now my thinking has changed to . . . because . . .<br>• My perspective about this topic changed when . . .</td></tr>
<tr><td colspan="2">Feedback: As Ms. Whitefeather observes groups, she notices that students can read and discuss facts, questions, and responses and identify what contributed to a change in their thinking. They still talk about one text and then move on to the next without pulling ideas from multiple sources. She gathers the whole group to share examples of its application of today's lesson and describes this next step.</td></tr>
</table>

continued →

<table>
<tr><td colspan="2">Lesson 3 learning target: I can pull together content from several sources sharing multiple perspectives on an issue and state in my own words.</td></tr>
<tr><td>Focus lesson and application of learning:<br>Ms. Whitefeather writes two questions to provoke students to synthesize their learning as they develop new perspectives. "As you read and watched video clips to learn more about this subject, what words, concepts, or ideas were brought up repeatedly? What are your own ideas and thinking about the subject?"<br><br>Next, Ms. Whitefeather provides one example of a big idea she gleaned from reading and watching videos on the topic. As she models, she points to important sentence stems and talking prompts that she generated. Students may use these prompts later as they work together in their groups. Her explanation includes the big idea, the rationale, and evidence to support her claim. She offers a new perspective as her thinking changed during her learning. Group members then may respond to her sharing. She releases students to articulate key ideas or themes and apply their new thinking, insights, and perspectives in their small-group discussions.</td><td>Sentence stems or question prompts:<br>• When I read or listened to . . . I gained insight about . . .<br>• This part in the article, story, or video challenged the assumptions I had about . . . My new thinking is . . .<br>• After considering all perspectives I most agree with . . .<br>• I want to use my new learning to . . .<br>• I feel compelled to do something and act on what I have now learned by . . .<br><br>Note: Before this lesson on synthesis of multiple sources, students will have read and gathered information and ideas from different individual articles or media sources. An FQR chart, Cornell Notes, or T-chart with headings labeled New Learning and My Thinking are tools students could use to help organize their ideas. (Cornell Notes is a focused note-taking method used to record and summarize key points and ideas during lecture, while reading, or while viewing or listening to media.)</td></tr>
<tr><td colspan="2">Feedback: Ms. Whitefeather meets with one to two groups and provides specific examples of how they synthesized during their discussions. As she observes and shares with these groups, she notices that they are relying on the literal and inferential explanation found within the texts and not yet connecting big ideas to other concepts, subjects, or their real-world experiences.</td></tr>
<tr><td colspan="2">Lesson 4 learning target: I can use information from a variety of sources, connect the important ideas with other ideas or concepts I have learned in other subjects or experiences I have had, and share them within my group to deepen its understanding about the topic.</td></tr>
<tr><td>Focus lesson and application of learning:<br>Ms. Whitefeather models how she might synthesize by sharing several important ideas from two or more different sources that she had written on sticky notes. Next, she organizes the notes by putting similar ideas together and then creates a heading that describes their contents for all to see. Then she thinks aloud, "What patterns do I see?" With this verbal prompt, she starts to synthesize the notes by combining the important ideas with her own thoughts, ideas, and experiences. As she thinks aloud, she connects the ideas to other concepts or subjects like mathematics or science, or maybe from a real-world experience she has encountered. Then, after she explains a new revelation, she writes one to two sentences that pull together all of her thinking. Finally, she shares some sentence stems that students may use as they share this process within their groups.</td><td>Sentence stems or question prompts:<br>• After thinking about the big ideas from these texts, what patterns can we see?<br>• How do the patterns found in these texts fit with our experiences and what we already know?<br>• What new learning do we have from combining the patterns in these texts to our experiences and what we know?<br>• A new way of looking at (big idea) is . . .<br>• A key idea derived from these texts is . . . I think we can sum up what this means using the word . . .</td></tr>
<tr><td colspan="2">Feedback: As Ms. Whitefeather observes and provides feedback to one to two groups, she notices that the group is doing well now with synthesizing multiple texts and sharing new thoughts during the discussion, but isn't consolidating the key ideas to bring closure to their discussion. Without this final synthesis, consensus around key points might not be reached and understanding may not be fully developed. Therefore, this learning and practice will serve as the focus of the next lesson.</td></tr>
</table>

| **Lesson 5 learning target:** I can identify and highlight key points discussed to synthesize and share new perspectives, thinking, and insight about a topic to bring closure to our discussion. | |
|---|---|
| **Focus lesson and application of learning:**<br>Ms. Whitefeather poses the following question for students to quickly turn and talk with a partner: "How can we keep track of topics or points that are heard repeatedly during discussion?"<br>As students are talking with partners, Ms. Whitefeather listens in and collects two to four ideas that were shared and asks these students to write their broad ideas on an anchor chart.<br>Together, as a class, they generate other ideas to add to the list of possible ways to keep track of key points, new ideas, and important discoveries made throughout the discussion. Then she shows a video clip where students highlight the key points of the discussion and offer several different ways to synthesize and bring closure to the lesson.<br>Ms. Whitefeather informs the class that she will tell them when there is five minutes left in discussion time so they won't have to worry about pacing this first time. Finally, she releases the class to use the resources they have been reading on a topic in the unit of study to discuss in small groups. | **Sentence stems or question prompts:**<br>• So, how can we apply this idea to our lives or another experience we have had?<br>• What key learning came from all of these texts?<br>• How might our thinking change based on . . .<br>• I have changed how I think about . . . based on . . .<br>• The idea in these articles about . . . is similar to an experience I had when . . .<br>• In the future, I am going to . . . as a result of my new thinking about . . .<br>• To synthesize our new learning and ideas, we discussed . . . and from that we learned . . . and the new way of looking at this one idea is . . . |
| **Feedback:** Ms. Whitefeather highlights the key points synthesized from one to two groups and specifically shares her observations with the larger group. She was impressed at these group members' synthesis of ideas shared to bring about a change in thinking after their in-depth discussion. She quickly highlights each group's strengths and asks students to keep better record of repeated points during discussion as these will lead the bigger ideas synthesis requires. | |

## Analyzing Students' Core Discussion Skills

In planning any curricular unit, designing a progression of lessons that builds on one another expands students' capacity to lead, facilitate, and propel discussion. The lesson progression includes at least three focus lessons during a unit of study for students to go deeper and sustain meaningful conversations.

Students' experiences, background knowledge, current beliefs, attitudes, and varying perspectives influence their interactions and discussions. A sixth-grade teacher planning a unit of study about multiple perspectives knows that several topics and issues may at times be controversial and challenge students' current perspectives. Although this may well be a desired outcome, the reality is that students struggle to take their discussion beyond surface-level exchanges because they aren't motivated or sure how to dig deeper or challenge others in productive, respectful ways.

Like anything else, you're going to get out of students what you're willing to put in. If students don't know specifically what you expect and are looking for during their discussions, you can anticipate flat, minor-league conversations to occur. You need to articulate the look-fors that will be used while observing and providing feedback during their discussions. This practice allows students to self-assess their own strengths and areas of growth—setting them up for major-league successes as self-directed learners!

Figure 6.5 features a rubric with three levels of performance—(1) developing, (2) approaching, and (3) arriving—that serve to more fully describe the core skills needed for rich, fruitful discussions. It is most useful for assisting with next steps in student development.

| Core Skills | Developing | Approaching | Arriving |
|---|---|---|---|
| Demonstrates independence and effective group behaviors | Has read the text and taken some notes with minimal organization | Has read text, taken notes, and generated some questions for discussion | Has read text, taken notes and organized them for quick access, and generated higher-level questions to propel discussion |
| | Comes prepared and sometimes contributes to discussion | Comes prepared and often contributes to discussion | Comes prepared and contributes greatly in a variety of ways to keep discussion flowing effectively |
| | Participation is not equally distributed as a speaker and listener; focuses on own contributions | Participation is fairly equally distributed as a speaker and listener | Treats others respectfully, shares talking time with others, and often draws other members into discussion |
| Builds strong content knowledge | Explores vocabulary but may not apply terms accurately | Inconsistently uses grade-level vocabulary | Consistently and accurately applies grade-level vocabulary |
| | Understands concepts | Understands grade-level concepts and applies them during discussion | Understands grade-level concepts and applies them in novel ways |
| | Beginning to ask questions but often doesn't ask them to extend discussion; sticks to initial perspective without changing after new ideas are generated | Asks questions, shares ideas, beginning to share new thinking when other ideas are offered; beginning to help others understand important concepts | Discusses ideas, questions others, negotiates meaning, clarifies and verbalizes new understanding, and makes ideas comprehensible to partners |
| Uses and adapts communication | Listens and connects to others with statements like, "I agree" or "I disagree" without further elaboration | Repeats what someone else says verbatim to highlight a point | Paraphrases to clarify, explain, or stay focused |
| | Uses short, brief sentences to make a point | When speaking, takes either a long time to make a point or there isn't enough of an explanation for members to see connection to topic | Speaks clearly and offers strong connections to topic; presents in an organized, concise, and interesting way |
| | Connections are made but not at the right time; reverts back to something said much earlier that causes discussion to go back to previous subtopic | Provides many ideas and talks often, but sometimes deviates from topic in order to speak | Often introduces a connecting subtopic which builds support for the subject; remains on topic |

**Figure 6.5:** Rubric of core skills used in discussions.

| | | | |
|---|---|---|---|
| Elaborates and asks others to expand on their ideas | As a speaker: Shares a general, complex, muddy, or abstract topic without much detail | Uses examples and some evidence from the text to explain ideas | Thoroughly and concisely explains ideas related to the topic with clarity through the use of strong connections, examples, analogies, textual evidence, or all of the above |
| | As a listener: Occasionally asks others to elaborate by saying, "Tell me more." | Randomly asks speaker to elaborate on specific point that needs clarification, "Can you elaborate on . . .?" | Asks the speaker to elaborate on key point that moves the conversation deeper, "Can you elaborate on the reasons why . . .?" |
| Cites evidence to support claims | Usually reads cited information directly from text or notes | Paraphrases and uses quotes accurately but may not add depth to conversation | Uses quotes as well as paraphrasing to cite textual evidence at appropriate times to add value to conversation and extend understanding |
| | Begins to challenge ideas but may not question evidence or questions evidence without judging its credibility | Challenges ideas | Appropriately judges examples of others and challenges ideas or evidence that do not provide strong, valid support |
| Synthesizes key points | May state both important as well as unimportant ideas to summarize ideas but doesn't add new thinking | Lists ideas talked about, provides a summary statement that includes ideas from multiple sources and new thinking | Remembers, highlights, and synthesizes key ideas from multiple sources used throughout the discussion and synthesizes comments, claims, and evidence made on all sides of an issue or topic in novel ways |

*Source: © 2016 by Sandi Novak.*

*Visit* ***go.SolutionTree.com/instruction*** *for a free reproducible version of this figure.*

Questioning, citing evidence, disagreeing, and synthesizing are critical skills and strategies needed for students to engage in deep academic discourse. While students are engaged in discussion, use a data-collection tool with look-fors as identified in the video viewing guides to monitor and record students' progress toward the learning target. Facilitating student-led discussions requires that you *step in* when needed to promote productivity and ensure students are focused on the content or topic. As important as it is to step in to assist students when needed, it is crucial that you remember to *step out* and let them go, in order for them to become self-directed learners.

All in all, you must remember that no matter the state or national standard that stimulates your planning, the possibilities you lead your students toward are expansive. Therefore, you must offer them skills and strategies for learning and for becoming more powerful. Student-led discussions help learners understand and make meaning of the world. By following the progression guides we suggest in this chapter, you can help your students move closer to the horizon where they learn and understand the world in deeper ways than ever before.

Chapter 6

# TAKE ACTION!

Use these reproducibles to apply your learning and, potentially, as a springboard for professional development work. Select three to four attributes in figure 6.5 (page 132) to assess your students' core discussion skills. For example: demonstrates independence and effective group behaviors, builds strong content knowledge, and uses and adapts communication. After observing students using the rubric, select one attribute to create a lesson progression that gets students to the end goal desired using the examples in chapter 6 as a guide. Determine the four to five learning targets needed in the progression and develop focus lessons and sentence stems from there.

Use the templates to create your lesson progressions.

| **Lesson progression 1 title:** | |
|---|---|
| Content learning target: | Speaking and listening learning target: |
| Focus lesson: | Sentence stems: |
| Look-fors or success indicators: | |

| **Lesson progression 2 title:** | |
|---|---|
| Content learning target: | Speaking and listening learning target: |
| Focus lesson: | Sentence stems: |
| Look-fors or success indicators: | |

| **Lesson progression 3 title:** | |
|---|---|
| Content learning target: | Speaking and listening learning target: |
| Focus lesson: | Sentence stems: |
| Look-fors or success indicators: | |

| **Lesson progression 4 title:** | |
|---|---|
| Content learning target: | Speaking and listening learning target: |
| Focus lesson: | Sentence stems: |
| Look-fors or success indicators: | |

chapter 7

# Pulling It All Together: Tools and Tips

*In younger grades, teachers want you to do group presentations. You freak out thinking about it. But as I get to talk more in discussions, I feel more comfortable expressing how I feel and think. It helps increase my confidence!*

—TAM, grade 9

The epigraphs in this book highlight various students expressing their opinions about leading and being involved in their own small-group discussions. Matthew (see page 153) tells us that it motivates him to read and contribute; Tam's confidence is built through small-group discussions; and Peter (see page 105) feels relieved to express his feelings. Certainly it comes as no surprise that students enjoy and look forward to opportunities where they can engage in meaningful conversations with their peers. However, we are aware of the challenges that sometimes arise in the process of developing and nurturing student conversations.

This chapter provides troubleshooting tips for teachers and then supplies administrators with the information and tools necessary to implement and sustain student-led discussions in every classroom throughout the school or district.

## Starting to Talk

Introducing the student-led discussion framework for the first time can feel overwhelming. It doesn't have to be. First, examine your current practice and look for student talk and discussion that you already have in place. You are already on your journey. Be confident in your new understandings and use your desire to incorporate more student-led discussions into your teaching as a springboard—and dive in! As with anything new, there will be successes, flops, challenges, and opportunities for improvement over time. Focus on a few key components as you begin, starting with classroom environment.

A classroom environment designed with student collaboration in mind is essential. Does the physical arrangement foster collaboration, interaction, and discussion? Are there gathering places for students to talk on a daily basis, including a space for whole-group learning, tables or desks arranged for small-group interaction, and spaces for partnership talk to occur?

Establish routines, procedures, and expectations to provide the structure for safe and meaningful discussions. What do respectful conversations look and sound like? What are teachers' responsibilities before, during, and after discussions and how can we help students hold each other accountable? Practice routines to build trust and community. This is a good place to start.

Model everything—never assume students know what to do or how to do it. Explicitly teach and model transitions from one space to another, how to share and respond during conversation, how to use text to support a claim or argument, and other skills and strategies that surface as you observe student discussions. Failure to model and establish the routines and structures necessary for student-led discussions will result in teacher and student frustration. With the first misstep, going back to old habits seems much easier than making the adjustments needed to sustain student talk. Resist this temptation. Model again, watch and analyze a video clip together, talk about what wasn't working, break the process down into smaller segments and focus lessons, see solutions, and try again.

Get students talking every day about their thinking, learning, and understandings. Switch it up so that discussions aren't predictable—provide different strategies in various groupings. During partner chats or small-group discussions, let students develop and ask their own questions. It would be easier to provide a prompt, clarify a misunderstanding, or give answers—don't! The communication and collaboration skills developed and reinforced in these moments will propel stronger student-led discussion later on. Deep learning and understanding result from students' struggling and dealing with challenges.

It is our natural inclination as educators to want to help students solve problems. Knowing our supporting nature, we can shift our thinking. Instead of solving their problems, we can assist them by providing solid, precise focus lessons with meaningful content, clear learning targets, and quality feedback. This combination strengthens student independence and confidence so that tackling real-world problems head-on becomes a comfortable habit for them.

## Troubleshooting Stalled or Derailed Discussions

Despite your best intentions and the time spent building relationships with students, carefully planning and designing lessons, establishing a classroom environment conducive for open discussion, and providing strong instruction, challenges are bound to surface before and during your journey toward student-led discussion. The issues we outline in the following sections are those troubleshooting topics that we have watched, experienced, and problem solved over the years. When you encounter them—and eventually you will—remember not to worry. These things happen to everyone from time to time, so use this as a strategic resource when necessary.

## Lack of Preparation

When a student arrives ill-equipped for a discussion, you might ponder, Why? Was the assignment too difficult? Does the student feel included and valued? Is he or she given a variety of safe ways to participate in class activities and discussions? Is the content compelling? Is there accountability?

Inquisitiveness about a topic and concern about what their classmates or teacher think serve as strong motivators for students to complete their assignments. Find out what makes that student tick. Provide choice in text selection. Ask him or her to help choose a topic or text for the content. Students are no different from anyone else. They will be prepared if they feel their work is valued and important.

Expect students to hold each other accountable and, together, develop ways to address and problem solve this issue when it arises. Do you currently have a system in place to help or support students in your class?

One common strategy that teachers use when students don't read text is to have them complete the reading assignment while others are involved in their discussions. Most students don't want to miss this opportunity to talk with their peers, so it often motivates them to get their reading done on time.

Haroon, a sixth-grade student, read his first chapter book ever in order to be part of a group discussion. Although there are many examples of students like Haroon, who are motivated to read because the discussions stimulate their curiosity and interest, this exclusion strategy doesn't work for all students. If students are not changing their reading habits after being kept out of a couple of discussions, try another approach. Remember, the goal is for students to be a part of the discussion.

## A Monopolizing Student

Engage the group in a conversation about participation and how to best include everyone's ideas and thoughts into a discussion. It is important to observe and note who is and is not talking during discussions. For those students who are doing most of the talking, suggest ways they might invite others into the conversation by providing sentence stems such as "(student's name), what are your ideas about . . .?"

Design focus or small-group lessons aimed at increasing student involvement with guided practice and feedback. Watch a video clip of a discussion where one student does a lot of the talking. Ask students for their ideas of how to help this student remember to share speaking time with others. Equip students with sentence starters or talking prompts that will help advocate for more balance in talking and listening opportunities. Use the talking chips strategy with groups that need help monitoring both speaking and listening during their discussion. English learners benefit from this strategy because it gives them a predictable format to share their thinking and a variety of examples to use as they craft a response.

In some of the videos we provide with this book, it may appear that one or two students dominate the discussion. Just as in adult group conversations, there are times when two people challenge a perspective which results in a back-and-forth exchange to clarify, elaborate, and question comments. This verbal volley between two people reminds us that we need to be careful not to make steadfast assumptions about students' group participation based on one short observation.

When students lead their own discussions they need to acquire and use decision-making and negotiation skills often not taught in our schools. Since they control the flow of their conversation, they need to ensure the participation of all group members. This skill, like all others, requires viewing good examples, having time to practice, and receiving specific feedback. Students may appear to struggle somewhat as they begin, but as they work within their groups all students become active listeners and speakers.

## Lack of Listening Skills

Chances are, if students aren't responding to each other or are responding inaccurately to others, they lack important listening skills. Have you explicitly taught and modeled active listening? Have you mentioned listening behaviors when you provided whole-group and individual feedback? After answering these questions, determine where you can revisit active listening with students. Video tape a student discussion and have students watch the video, take notes, and self-assess their own listening. Once students have identified areas of need, help them draft a plan for improvement, such as implementing a note-taking strategy while others are talking or paraphrasing what another group member has said, instead of introducing a new thought or idea.

## Conversations Lack Substance

Students are grouped into pairs, triads, or small groups and they are having conversations. Initially, one student begins talking and others respond with comments or generally agree with the speaker. Soon after, another student jumps in to share a new thought or idea and the pattern continues. These types of conversations frequently occur in classrooms. A good amount of talking occurs, but the rigor, depth, and development of new insights are lacking.

You can increase your students' capacity to engage in meaningful, deep discussions if you:

- Equip them with a variety of interesting texts or media that address meaningful content with purposeful outcomes

- Provide consistently scheduled periods of time for conversation that are long enough to allow for deep conversations to develop
- Explicitly teach clusters of focus lessons as described in chapter 6 (page 105)

These adjustments help develop student stamina and increase their probability of success. And, as we all know, success breeds success!

Students want to know that their learning serves a greater purpose. Why is what they are learning important? What results can they anticipate from their new understandings? Could it be used to teach or inform others? Could they share and connect with the local community or the world? Might they use their knowledge to resolve an issue in the school? Allowing students to create and connect with a topic gives them more ownership and more to say.

Student-led discussion requires stamina and consistent opportunities for practice. Schedule discussions (partner chats and small groups) into your lesson plans. Embed turn-and-talks into your focus lesson or to close the day's learning. Although these quick conversations engage and excite students, the longer, small-group discussions offer a structure for the application and synthesis of learning. Just like independent reading, gradually increasing the duration of student discussions over time is essential. In third grade and beyond, it often takes twenty to thirty minutes for students to get to deep academic discourse in a discussion. Although we may not have enough time daily to devote to these student-led, small-group discussions, scheduling longer periods two to three times a week will enhance and strengthen student learning.

Using probing questions and citing textual evidence propels discussions to a deeper level. Some questions elicit the deep and rigorous discussions that translate into learning. Make certain students know which questions enhance discussion and create thinking and reflection among group members. Begin by having students create and use questions requiring deep thinking that they generate while reading. Students will have more opportunities to practice if they begin their practice of asking questions with partners before working in small groups.

From there, observe and record the types of questions students generate with their partners. Are they responding and building new questions as they talk? Notice how the listener responds to the question. Does the student redirect with another question, make a comment, or pause to think and then respond? A good question does not have an expedient answer. Rather, it stimulates critical thinking. Getting students to explain and expand their thinking is always a challenge. Design focus lessons to specifically address these skills. Guide students to develop an idea or two from their conversations, first in writing and then talk about them with a partner. This is often referred to as *blowing up a sentence* or *an idea* in writing class and provides the detail necessary to strengthen the writing for the reader.

Well-structured probing questions require the speaker to expand and explain his or her thinking or substantiate an argument. Often, gathering and interpreting new evidence is needed for this expanded thinking to happen. If not already being used, post anchor charts with question stems for students to refer to during discussion. These supports, which aid and reinforce the flow of conversation, can be used until students are able to apply the skills on their own.

## Difficulty Providing Feedback

Presenting students with feedback that is timely and specific is critical to move students along the discussion continuum. During your observation of student discussions make sure to collect evidence specific to the learning targets of your focus lesson or those skills students have been practicing. When conferring with students, share specific instances from their conversation that were done well and those skills that need to be refined moving forward. Specific feedback, designed to improve student learning and performance, is motivating. Students want to get better—praise strengths, offer guidance, and follow up with opportunities to practice the targeted skills identified.

Use one of the note-taking formats provided in chapter 3 (page 43), or create your own. Keeping accurate notes helps provide specific feedback and document your students' discussion journey.

## Lack of Interest in a Text or Topic

Have you ever read something you couldn't put down or had to stop reading right in the middle of an article you couldn't wait to finish? High-interest and challenging texts can be the catalyst for excellent student discussions. Similarly, controversial topics and current events can propel discussion. Select texts and topics that stimulate students to form opinions, have relevance, or encourage them to examine their own lives. Passion drives high-level questions, disagreements, and the skills needed to create and sustain meaningful discussions. Offering students different types of text and access to multiple sources strengthens their desire to read and improve discussions. Although students must be able to read and comprehend text, don't underestimate their ability and drive to decipher complex text when they *want* to read it. Additionally, working in a group helps all students better understand the meaning of complex text.

Content standards and the lesson's purpose drive text selection. For example, if the learning target in a language arts class requires students to analyze and evaluate an argument and specific claims, the teacher should choose a high-interest topic with opposing views represented in the text. Often, current events or text related to their personal lives are perfect selections to engage students while working toward mastery of the learning target.

A question you might still be wondering about is, "How do I engage a student that just doesn't want to engage, be there, contribute, or do anything you or their discussion group desires?" First and foremost, we must remember that we cannot control what is happening outside our classroom walls, however, we have an obligation to each student in our school or classroom to assist with his or her social and academic learning.

If presented with a similar situation, the first approach would be to find out what is going on in that student's mind.

Why doesn't he or she want to engage? A quick conversation, note, sticky note, or peer might all be helpful if this occurs. If you then determine an outside factor is getting in the way of the student's learning, acknowledge where the student is and how he or she is feeling. Work alongside these students to get started and contribute in some way during that day's class. The possibilities are unlimited, but here are a few ideas.

- Record their group's discussion to show and review later.
- Provide a prompt or question for them to share during discussion or to begin their work.
- Listen in on a different group's discussion for the day and contribute at will.
- Listen for and take notes about the main content idea or learning target for that day.

Most students will respect you for taking an interest in them rather than seeing them as someone who doesn't care or doesn't want to be there. Likewise, if you are able to determine that the topic is of zero interest, the reading or task is too difficult or long, or they are having trouble with one or more group members, listen to what they are saying and work with them to provide choices in what or how they tackle the activity or discussion. Choice does not mean they don't have to do anything. Be firm and hold them accountable while modifying and adjusting in order for that individual, you, and the class to progress.

# Establishing a Whole-School Approach

An individual teacher's effort to provide effective student-led discussions can certainly propel student learning. However, more than one year of instruction from just a single teacher is usually required to bring students to high levels of proficiency in facilitating their own discussions as well as developing strong communication and group behavior skills. To have the strongest effect on student development, teachers should look to the school as the unit of change, and leaders should organize professional development to promote teacher learning that leads to a coherent, schoolwide approach.

This section provides tools, resources, and guidance for school leaders to develop a whole-school or district culture where students receive multiple opportunities throughout the day to engage in enriched student-led discussions.

## Common Queries

Leaders want to know what they can do to promote quality student-led, small-group interactions in their *whole* school. School district administrators are curious about what they would see as they conduct walkthroughs if student-led discussions were part of the school culture—and more importantly, how student-led discussions would transform schools and achievement.

Some teachers don't know where or how to begin. A few others have tried student-led discussions in their classrooms, but their attempts have not been very successful. These teachers want to remedy the cause of their frustrations but need help determining what went wrong. Many other teachers report using small-group discussions, but deep discourse rarely occurs or occurs only in the groups with the most capable students. The section Troubleshooting Stalled or Derailed Discussions (page 138) provides responses to common pitfalls encountered when implementing student-led discussions in classrooms and other ponderings when teachers think about what could be.

## Current Status

Leaders need to assess current practices; determine strengths and needs; explore the resources, professional development and support needed; and plan for ways to improve whether implementing student-led discussions in a classroom, grade level, school, or district. Best results usually come from creating a well-conceived and thoroughly communicated plan.

Gathering data is essential before implementing a change in practice and instruction, and student-led discussions are no different. We developed three resources to assist in assembling these data: (1) a *teacher self-assessment* centered on indicators needed for student-led discussions to flourish, (2) a *student survey* that asks students about their classroom environment and practices related to student-led discussions, and (3) a *classroom visit observation instrument* that provides data on educational practices throughout the school related to student-led discussion criteria.

### *Teacher Self-Assessment*

A teacher self-assessment (figure 7.1) allows each teacher to reflect on his or her own understanding and use of instructional practices related to student discussions. Initially, leaders can use this resource to provide baseline data to determine needs that will be addressed through professional learning or added resources. Principals, professional development staff, and teacher leaders can also use it to guide professional learning, planning, and implementation.

### *Student Survey*

Student reflection and reporting assists learning and growth—for both students and teachers. A student survey (figure 7.2, page 147) can provide students with a chance to tell teachers what current practices exist in classrooms from their perspective, while providing school leaders with information to plan next steps.

**Directions:** Rate your current level of understanding and use of the following practices to promote student-led discussions by selecting one option from the Understanding column and one option from the Use column for each item.

| Description | Understanding | | | | | Use | | | | |
|---|---|---|---|---|---|---|---|---|---|---|
| | No understanding | Limited understanding | Developing understanding | Good understanding | Expert understanding | Rarely or never use or do | Use or do one to two times per year | Use or do one to two times per month | Use or do one to two times per week | Use or do daily |
| 1. Have students read self-selected books independently in the classroom. | | | | | | | | | | |
| 2. Create a classroom environment conducive for student-led discussions. | | | | | | | | | | |
| 3. Establish rituals and routines to ensure students can discuss on their own. | | | | | | | | | | |
| 4. Explicitly teach and model grade-level speaking and listening standards. | | | | | | | | | | |
| 5. Use a variety of formats to engage students in discussion. | | | | | | | | | | |
| 6. Use a variety of grouping configurations for students to practice their speaking and listening skills. | | | | | | | | | | |
| 7. Have students prepare for discussions by reading the text and taking discussion-worthy notes. | | | | | | | | | | |
| 8. Develop both content and speaking and listening learning targets. | | | | | | | | | | |
| 9. Select text that stimulates discussion-worthy topics. | | | | | | | | | | |
| 10. Explicitly teach and model both content and speaking and listening learning targets. | | | | | | | | | | |
| 11. Have student engage in small-group, student-led discussions about texts or important topics. | | | | | | | | | | |
| 12. Record data while observing students applying the learning targets during discussions. | | | | | | | | | | |

continued →

**Figure 7.1:** Student-led discussions teacher self-assessment.

| Description | Understanding | | | | | Use | | | | |
|---|---|---|---|---|---|---|---|---|---|---|
| | No understanding | Limited understanding | Developing understanding | Good understanding | Expert understanding | Rarely or never use or do | Use or do one to two times per year | Use or do one to two times per month | Use or do one to two times per week | Use or do daily |
| 13. Provide feedback to students on their application of both content and speaking and listening learning targets. | | | | | | | | | | |
| 14. Plan a cluster of lessons around a particular topic or important strategy that progresses in complexity. | | | | | | | | | | |
| 15. Explicitly teach a cluster of lessons that develop students' speaking and listening skills and align with grade-level standards. | | | | | | | | | | |
| 16. Help students engage in discussions that result in deep academic discourse. | | | | | | | | | | |
| 17. Students assume considerable responsibility for the discussion's success. | | | | | | | | | | |
| 18. Students ensure all voices are heard in the discussion. | | | | | | | | | | |
| 19. Students formulate and use their own questions to propel discussion. | | | | | | | | | | |

*Source: © 2016 by Sandi Novak.*

*Visit* ***go.SolutionTree.com/instruction*** *for a free reproducible version of this figure.*

### *Classroom Visit Observation Instrument*

A classroom visit observation instrument enables observers to record information over time on features of student-led discussions. Data gathered from the whole school highlights the elements of student-led discussions that are already happening and those areas needing more development. Through the use of this data-collection tool, the current reality of teacher instruction and student learning is collected and analyzed. Use this instrument to make an initial determination of the current status of the instructional elements and student behaviors listed on the form after teachers have taken the teacher survey and know that the school's focus will be on providing more opportunities for students to speak throughout the day. Later, after providing professional learning, use it to look for implementation. Video 7.1 "Using the Classroom Visit Instrument" shows a leadership group conducting classroom visits using an instrument

**Directions:** Circle the correct response to each item.

## Student Survey About Discussions

1. In which classes do you participate in discussions?
   a. Reading or writing
   b. Mathematics
   c. Science
   d. Social studies
   e. Specials
   f. Other: ______________________
2. Who typically leads your discussions?
   a. Students
   b. Teacher
3. What group size do you meet in?
   a. Pairs (two)
   b. Triads (three)
   c. Small groups (four to six)
   d. Whole group
4. Who does most of the talking in your classroom?
   a. Teacher
   b. Students
5. Do you feel discussion increases your understanding about a topic or content area?
   a. Definitely
   b. Sometimes
   c. Rarely
   d. Never
6. How many times *a day* do you engage in discussion with other students about your learning?
   a. 0–1
   b. 2–4
   c. 4–6
   d. 7 or more
7. The teacher posts anchor charts or posters to help me during discussions.
   a. Always
   b. Usually
   c. Sometimes
   d. Never
8. I use anchor charts or posters to help me during discussions.
   a. Always
   b. Usually
   c. Sometimes
   d. Never
9. I feel that I have the skills needed for my discussions with others.
   a. Always
   b. Usually
   c. Sometimes
   d. Never
10. I feel confident during discussions with other students.
    a. Always
    b. Usually
    c. Sometimes
    d. Never
11. My teacher has provided targeted lessons about what a good discussion looks like.
    a. Yes
    b. No
12. I have watched and learned from other students engaged in discussions.
    a. Yes
    b. No
13. My teacher takes notes during our discussion and talks about ways we can get better.
    a. Always
    b. Usually
    c. Sometimes
    d. Never
14. I know what I am supposed to do before, during, and after my discussion.
    a. Always
    b. Usually
    c. Sometimes
    d. Never

continued →

**Figure 7.2:** Student survey about discussions.

| For each question number, select the choice that best reflects how you feel during discussions. | | | |
|---|---|---|---|
| 15. | a. Excited | b. Okay | c. Bored |
| 16. | a. Prepared | b. Sometimes prepared | c. Confused |
| 17. | a. Included | b. Included with some students | c. Left out |
| 18. | a. Like to talk in my group | b. Sometimes like to talk in my group | c. Don't like to talk in my group |

*Source:* © *2016 by Cara Slattery.*

*Visit* ***go.SolutionTree.com/instruction*** *for a free reproducible version of this figure.*

that focuses on indicators of effective student-led discussions to determine the status of releasing more learning to students through discussions.

Read through each component of the classroom visit observation instrument prior to conducting walkthroughs to become familiar with the tool. Watch a few of the videos included in this book, including video 7.1, to practice recording observations prior to going into classrooms. Watch and observe, place check marks or the designated letters to reflect what is observed during the visit. Remember, this is a quick snapshot of many classrooms, so the observer cannot assume certain things did or did not occur before or after the visit. This is not an assessment of an individual or classroom, but rather an instrument to assist a school or district in identifying trends and guiding next steps.

Leaders can customize the classroom visit observation instrument for the school by entering the grades or classes across the top. In figure 7.3, the elementary school has two sections of kindergarten, three sections of first grade, two sections of second and third grades, and one section for each of grades 4 and 5. Create additional columns if more sections are required.

The observer visits a classroom for three to five minutes and identifies all components, or look-fors, found in the classroom by placing a check mark in the appropriate space. For example, the observer might place a check mark in the first third-grade column of the row corresponding to *sentence stems or talking prompts are displayed*, if that was observed in that particular classroom on the day of the observation. It's possible that the observer may not check the second third-grade column of the same item related to sentence stems if he or she did not see sentence stems in that classroom. In this case, the space remains empty.

After gathering all data, administrators and teacher leaders can determine strengths and areas of need to determine a plan of action. A systematic change in practice will only be as successful as the time, talent, and passion behind it.

## Professional Learning

Professional development for student-led discussions requires more than one or two sit-and-get sessions. Initially, plan to explain why student-led discussions are important, how they will improve student learning and achievement, and provide staff with an outline of the structures that must be present in a classroom where successful

| Classroom Visits: Looking for Student-Led Discussions Framework | | | | | | | | | | | |
|---|---|---|---|---|---|---|---|---|---|---|---|
| **Classroom** | **K** | **K** | **1** | **1** | **1** | **2** | **2** | **3** | **3** | **4** | **5** |
| **Classroom Environment** | | | | | | | | | | | |
| The desks are arranged in groups or tables are used. | | | | | | | | | | | |
| Anchor charts are displayed with speaking and listening assistance as well as content. | | | | | | | | | | | |
| There is a rich collection of texts (300+) in the classroom library. | | | | | | | | | | | |
| Sentence stems or talking prompts are displayed. | | | | | | | | | | | |
| **Method of Instruction** **(W = whole group; S = small group; C = conferring)** | | | | | | | | | | | |
| **Learning Targets** | | | | | | | | | | | |
| Content learning target is posted in student-friendly language. | | | | | | | | | | | |
| Speaking and listening learning target is posted in student-friendly language. | | | | | | | | | | | |
| Learning target is taught and monitored in whole-group, small-group, or in independent work. | | | | | | | | | | | |
| **Focus Lesson** | | | | | | | | | | | |
| Teacher is explicitly teaching or modeling content learning target. | | | | | | | | | | | |
| Teacher is explicitly teaching or modeling speaking and listening learning target. | | | | | | | | | | | |
| Teacher is giving whole-group feedback on learning target or discussion skills. | | | | | | | | | | | |
| Students are listening, engaged, and interacting with peers. | | | | | | | | | | | |
| Students are listening, engaged, and interacting with teacher. | | | | | | | | | | | |
| **Small Group** | | | | | | | | | | | |
| Teacher is leading students' discussion and strategy application. | | | | | | | | | | | |
| Teacher is observing students as they discuss in their groups. | | | | | | | | | | | |
| Teacher is recording notes as students discuss in their groups. | | | | | | | | | | | |
| Teacher is giving feedback to students about their application of learning target. | | | | | | | | | | | |
| Students are talking about text or topic with a partner. | | | | | | | | | | | |
| Students are discussing in small groups. | | | | | | | | | | | |
| Students are practicing the learning target modeled and taught in focus lesson. | | | | | | | | | | | |
| No student discussion is observed. | | | | | | | | | | | |

continued →

**Figure 7.3:** Student-led discussion framework classroom visit instrument.

| Classroom | K | K | 1 | 1 | 1 | 2 | 2 | 3 | 3 | 4 | 5 |
|---|---|---|---|---|---|---|---|---|---|---|---|
| **Independent Work and Application** | | | | | | | | | | | |
| Teacher is conferring with student and providing feedback about learning target. | | | | | | | | | | | |
| Students are reading and applying learning target. | | | | | | | | | | | |
| Students are recording notes related to learning target. | | | | | | | | | | | |
| **Student Input** | | | | | | | | | | | |
| Student can explain the learning target, skill, or strategy. | | | | | | | | | | | |
| Student knows his or her specific goal—*personal communication skills.* | | | | | | | | | | | |
| Each student reports the last time he or she discussed with a group was (1) today, (2) this week, (3) last week, (4) this month, or (5) longer. | | | | | | | | | | | |

*Source: Adapted from Houck & Novak, 2016.*

*Visit* ***go.SolutionTree.com/instruction*** *to download a free reproducible version of this figure.*

discussions are happening. This might be a perfect time to introduce a couple of books for book studies about student-led discussions and give opportunities to watch video clips of students and teachers in action. Knowing ahead of time what great student-led discussions look and sound like provides a schema for teachers when beginning or learning more about this practice. This approach solidifies the *what* and the *why* before moving into the *how*.

Modeling for teachers is just as critical as it is for students. Many teachers have not been in a classroom environment where leading and sustaining small-group discussions are the students' responsibilities. Ways to shift school culture to increase the use of this instructional approach might include modeling during group meetings, showing video clips followed by adult small-group discussions, providing opportunities to observe classrooms where discussions are in full swing, or conducting group meetings that alternate among a variety of discussion formats.

Discussions are job-embedded and therefore need to be integrated into what teachers are already doing. It isn't an add-on. Instead, it's a change in practice. Gradually, as we've covered throughout this book, instruction shifts, focus lessons follow a progression, and students assume more of their own learning and deeper learning occurs. Give time and patience for moving forward with discussions and trust that the results will be transformative.

Even with the best-laid plan, pitfalls and challenges will arise during implementation. We don't want these obstacles to lead to frustration and abandonment of a transformative instructional practice. Anticipating what may happen and providing guidance and suggestions for overcoming challenges helps teachers feel supported while moving along the learning and teaching continuum.

Chapter 7

# TAKE ACTION!

Use this reproducible to apply your learning and, potentially, as a springboard for professional development work.

1. Administer the *Teacher Self-Assessment* survey and the *Student Survey* to determine the status of student-led discussions in the school.

| Whole-School Action Plan | | | | |
|---|---|---|---|---|
| Goal | Activity | Steps to Implement Activity | Person Responsible | How Success Will Be Determined |
| | | | | |
| | | | | |
| | | | | |

2. After reviewing the data from the teacher and student data-collection resources, determine the professional learning and resources needed to increase student-led discussions throughout the school.

| Individual Teacher Action Plan | | | | |
|---|---|---|---|---|
| Goal | Activity | Steps to Implement Activity | Person Responsible | How Success Will Be Determined |
| | | | | |
| | | | | |
| | | | | |

3. After reflecting on the Whole-School Action Plan, teachers complete the Individual Teacher Action Plan either individually or as a collaborative grade-level team.

# Conclusion

*Since it's more comfortable to talk in a group, you usually say more, go deeper in a topic, and get to hear different points of view. Discussing in groups makes you more curious and makes reading more exciting. It's more of a motivation to read.*

—MATTHEW, grade 9

Can student talk increase motivation? Does it develop speaking and listening skills? Will it make learning content standards more exciting? Might it help students become better readers, writers, critical thinkers, and problem solvers? Are students able to take ownership of their learning during their discussions? Will it increase student achievement? Without a doubt, the answer is *yes* to each question. Students are desperate to become active in their own learning, collaborate with each other, and have a little fun in the process!

We believe the student-led discussion framework contributes to establishing a culture conducive to 21st century learning in four important ways. First, this framework highlights the importance of combining content and communication standards. The examples used throughout the book provide ways to more purposefully teach these important speaking and listening skills, together with content, and have students apply them when they converse with their peers.

Second, the student-led discussion framework provides a point of interest to begin sustained professional work for whole-school efforts aimed at higher standards for literacy, teaching, and learning. Sometimes it's difficult to find a broad instructional and student learning area in need of growth that brings teachers from kindergarten through high school to the table with the same high levels of interest. Yet, students in all grades can benefit from leading their own discussions.

Third, this framework provides a responsible approach in preparing students for a world where communication is an important fundamental skill in any career or job. Learning through discussions is an active process requiring many skills and strategies to work simultaneously. Students read to acquire knowledge, ask questions to fulfill their curiosities, offer evidence to support their positions or claims, gain new personal insights, and understand alternative perspectives when they hear ideas and opinions that don't resonate with their own.

As educators, we can plan a structure for our lessons, guide students as they prepare, and provide feedback, but we can't plan the conversation itself or script the learning. Students drive the thinking, which presents limitless possibilities. When students are engaged in conversation about content, their questions, insights, and challenges inspire new learning and inquiry. Student learning deepens, and they bring meaning to each other in ways we, as teachers, cannot.

Fourth, using this framework gives students more ownership and responsibility for their learning and they enjoy it more. In *The Global Achievement Gap*, author Tony Wagner (2010) writes, "My interviews with students as well as with high school and college teachers, confirm that students are increasingly impatient with the lecture style of teaching and the reliance on textbooks for information, and crave more discussion" (p. 178).

Chances are you chose to read this book because you wanted to increase the number of student-led discussions in your classroom or you aspire to learn new techniques to enhance your students' skills, engagement, or motivation. The examples and videos we share in this book should inspire you to explore the potential of providing more of these opportunities for your students. The video clips show real teachers and students involved in student-led discussions, and the effect these discussions have on students' understanding is evident.

We know that student-led discussions don't just happen. They require systems and structures that provide consistency and accountability. Students first develop positive relationships with each other and feel safe to take risks and share in an academic setting. For discussions to succeed, preparation and participation from all group members must be expected and valued.

As educators, we expose students to all types of text and media to engage and inform them as they compare, contrast, and synthesize their understanding. For student-led discussions to be successful, they cannot be something students get to do just once in a while. Instead, they must be built into our schedules and routines—predictable and permanent—with the conversation being viewed as critical as the content or text itself. Student talk develops reasoning about a variety of topics, leading to deeper understanding while building communication competencies. Students learn to see beyond themselves and view the world from multiple perspectives.

Using this framework and giving students more opportunities to speak can provide benefits to schools, teachers, and students. Schools benefit with an outcome of purposeful and planned instruction targeting *communication* and *group functioning*. Through this transformation in instruction, students learn how to communicate ideas in a variety of formats and also how to interact with a wide range of people in academic settings. With a whole-school focus on providing more voice to students, it becomes a dynamic and exciting place where student learning takes center stage.

Teachers benefit in the opportunity to improve instruction and to purposefully teach speaking and listening standards. Teachers will also appreciate the difference that student-led discussion can make in student engagement and sustained learning. Furthermore, they will be pleased about improved on-task behavior resulting from successful implementation.

For students, they will learn more, build their confidence, develop an appreciation of other perspectives, and improve their retention if they regularly converse with their peers. It also helps them refine or extend their repertoire of speaking and listening skills. Through discussion, students reflect on and assess their own learning, plan next steps, and *apply their learning in novel ways*—the ultimate learning goal. Discussion also builds the cognitively engaging classrooms that they crave.

Our intent in presenting this topic is not to imply that student-led discussions are always preferable to teacher-led discussions. Teachers sometimes need to direct the content and flow of a class discussion. Our appeal is to make these inquiry-oriented discussions more integral practices in all classrooms. Students will benefit from opportunities to discuss their own perspectives of topics and texts they are reading. Leading their own discussions enables them to explore an endless domain of possibilities, deepen their thinking about the world in which they live, and own the love of learning. In these types of discussions, students must assume responsibility for the content they explore, the direction their conversation takes, and negotiating the outcomes.

Many students don't come to school equipped with these skills and they don't just develop naturally on their own. Providing instructional support that focuses on content and discussion skills while gradually releasing responsibility to students will strengthen engagement, and learning will soar. Together, appropriate instruction and abundant opportunities to practice will result in deep academic discourse among our students who become fully prepared for college and their careers. Isn't that what we all strive to accomplish?

A sixth-grade student sums it up best when she says, "We should have more time to talk about the things we are reading. I have something to say but don't unless I work with others in my group" (A. Quest, personal communication, April 2013). A ninth grader wants you to know, "Members of your group are not judgmental. You don't have to worry about what they are going to think about you. You don't have to be afraid to talk. They listen to you, so you talk more!" (A. Barnes, personal communication, October 2015).

All students should be given ample opportunities for their voices to be heard in our classrooms. Let's let our students talk! We will laugh, cry, and remember why we became educators when our encouragement of deep discourse lets them engage in purposeful, significant student-led discussions.

# Appendix: List of Videos

# References

Allington, R. L. (2006). *What really matters for struggling readers: Designing research-based programs* (2nd ed.). Boston: Pearson.

Allington, R. L., & Gabriel, R. E. (2012). Every child, every day. *Educational Leadership, 69*(6), 10–15.

Almasi, J. F., McKeown, M. G., & Beck, I. L. (1996). The nature of engaged reading in classroom discussions of literature. *Journal of Literacy Research, 28*(1), 107–146.

Almasi, J. F., O'Flahavan, J. F., & Arya, P. (2001). A comparative analysis of student and teacher development in more and less proficient discussions of literature. *Reading Research Quarterly, 36*(2), 96–120.

American Association for the Advancement of Science. (1993). *Benchmarks for science literacy: A tool for curriculum reform.* New York: Oxford University Press.

American Association for the Advancement of Science. (2001a). *Atlas of science literacy: Mapping K–12 science learning* (vol. 1). Washington, DC: Author.

American Association for the Advancement of Science. (2001b). *Atlas of science literacy: Mapping K–12 science learning* (vol. 2). Washington, DC: Author.

Anderson, R. D. (2002). Reforming science teaching: What research says about inquiry. *Journal of Science Teacher Education, 13*(1), 1–12.

Angelou, M. (1978). Still I rise. In *And still I rise.* New York: Random House. Accessed at www.poets.org/poetsorg/poem/still-i-rise on April 1, 2016.

Applebee, A. N. (2003). *The language of literature.* New York: McDougal.

Applegate, K. (2007). *Home of the brave.* New York: Feiwel and Friends.

Avci, S., & Yuksel, A. (2011). Cognitive and affective contributions of the literature circles method on the acquisition of reading habits and comprehension skills in primary level students. *Educational Sciences: Theory and Practice, 11*(3), 1295–1300.

Ball, D. L. (1993). With an eye on the mathematical horizon: Dilemmas of teaching elementary school mathematics. *Elementary School Journal, 93*(4), 373–397.

Balliett, B. (2013). *Hold fast.* New York: Scholastic.

Berry, R. A. W., & Englert, C. S. (2005). Designing conversation: Book discussions in a primary inclusion classroom. *Learning Disability Quarterly, 28*(1), 35–58.

Bowen, C. W. (2000). A quantitative literature review of cooperative learning effects on high school and college chemistry achievement. *Journal of Chemical Education, 77*(1), 116–119.

Bransford, J. D., Brown, A. L., Cocking, R. R., & National Research Council Committee on Developments in the Science of Learning. (2000). *How people learn: Brain, mind, experience, and school: Expanded edition.* Washington, DC: National Academy Press.

Brett, J. (2010). *The 3 little Dassies.* New York: Putnam's.

Brookhart, S. M. (2008). *How to give effective feedback to your students.* Alexandria, VA: Association for Supervision and Curriculum Development.

Brookhart, S. M. (2012). Preventing feedback fizzle. *Educational Leadership, 70*(1), 24–29.

Brooks, J. G. (2002). *Schooling for life: Reclaiming the essence of learning.* Alexandria, VA: Association for Supervision and Curriculum Development.

Brooks, J. G. (2011). *Big science for growing minds: Constructivist classrooms for young thinkers.* New York: Teachers College Press.

Bruner, J. (1977). *The process of education: A landmark in educational theory* (Rev. ed.). Cambridge, MA: Harvard University Press.

Byrd, J. (2008). *Guidebook for student-centered classroom discussions.* Parkersburg, WV: Interactivity Foundation.

Cai, J., & Lester, F. (2010). *Why is teaching with problem solving important to student learning?* National Council of Teachers of Mathematics Problem Solving Research Brief. Accessed at www.nctm.org/uploadedFiles/Research_and_Advocacy/research_brief_and_clips/Research_brief_14_-_Problem_Solving.pdf?%20Target= on August 13, 2016.

Cameron, S., Murray, M., Hull, K., & Cameron, J. (2012). Engaging fluent readers using literature circles. *Literacy Learning: The Middle Years, 20*(1), 1–8.

Cecil, N. L. (1995). *The art of inquiry: Questioning strategies for K–6 classrooms.* Winnipeg, Canada: Peguis.

Certo, J., Moxley, K., Reffitt, K., & Miller, J. A. (2010). "I learned how to talk about a book": Children's perceptions of literature circles across grade and ability levels. *Literacy Research and Instruction, 49*(3), 243–263.

Chapin, S. H., O'Connor, C., & Anderson, N. C. (2009). *Classroom discussion: Using math talk to help students learn, grades K–6.* Sausalito, CA: Math Solutions.

Chappuis, J. (2012). How am I doing? *Educational Leadership, 70*(1), 36–41.

Christoph, J. N., & Nystrand, M. (2001). Taking risks, negotiating relationships: One teacher's transition towards a dialogic classroom. *Research in the Teaching of English, 36*(2), 249–286.

Cirillo, M. (2013). *What does research say the benefits of discussion in mathematics class are?* Reston, VA: National Council of Teachers of Mathematics.

Coleman, D., & Pimentel, S. (2012). *Revised publishers' criteria for the Common Core State Standards in English language arts and literacy, grades 3–12.* Accessed at www.corestandards.org/assets/Publishers_Criteria_for_3-12.pdf on April 1, 2016.

Combs, B. (2015). The Confederate battle flag is a symbol of intimidation [Opinion]. *New York Times.* Accessed at www.nytimes.com/roomfordebate/2015/06/19/does-the-confederate-flag-breed-racism/the-confederate-battle-flag-is-a-symbol-of-intimidation on April 1, 2016.

Copeland, M. (2014). *Life in motion: An unlikely ballerina—My story of adversity and grace.* New York: Touchstone.

Daniels, H. (2002). *Literature circles: Voice and choice in book clubs and reading groups.* Portland, ME: Stenhouse Publishers.

Danielson, C. (1996). *Enhancing professional practice: A framework for teaching.* Alexandria, VA: Association for Supervision and Curriculum Development.

Danielson, C. (2007). *Enhancing professional practice: A framework for teaching* (2nd ed.). Alexandria, VA: Association for Supervision and Curriculum Development.

Davis, E. A., & Miyake, N. (Eds.). (2004). Scaffolding. *The Journal of the Learning Sciences, 13*(3), 265–272.

Dean, C. B., Hubbell, E. R., Pitler, H., & Stone, B. (2012). *Classroom instruction that works: Research-based strategies for increasing student achievement* (2nd ed.). Alexandria, VA: Association for Supervision and Curriculum Development.

de Garcia, L. A. (n.d.). *How to get students talking! Generating math talk that supports math learning.* Accessed at www.mathsolutions.com/documents/how_to_get_students_talking.pdf on April 1, 2016.

Duschl, R. A., Schweingruber, H. A., & Shouse, A. W. (Eds.). (2007). *Taking science to school: Learning and teaching science in grades K–8.* Washington, DC: National Academy Press.

Edwards, M. C., & Edelen, M. O. (2009). Special topics in item response theory. In R. Millsap & A. Maydeu-Olivares (Eds.), *The SAGE handbook of quantitative methods in psychology* (pp. 178–198). Los Angeles: SAGE.

Elias, M. J. (2006). The connection between academic and social-emotional learning. In M. J. Elias & H. A. Arnold (Eds.), *The educator's guide to emotional intelligence and academic achievement: Social-emotional learning in the classroom* (pp. 4–14). Thousand Oaks, CA: Corwin Press.

Fisher, D., & Frey, N. (2007). *Checking for understanding: Formative assessment techniques for your classroom.* Alexandria, VA: Association for Supervision and Curriculum Development.

Fisher, D., Frey, N., & Lapp, D. (2012). *Text complexity: Raising rigor in reading.* Newark, DE: International Reading Association.

Fisher, D., Frey, N., & Rothenberg, C. (2008). *Content-area conversations: How to plan discussion-based lessons for diverse language learners.* Alexandria, VA: Association for Supervision and Curriculum Development.

Fountas, I. C., & Pinnell, G. S. (1996). *Guided reading: Good first teaching for all children.* Portsmouth, NH: Heinemann.

Frey, N., Fisher, D., & Everlove, S. (2009). *Productive group work: How to engage students, build teamwork, and promote understanding.* Alexandria, VA: Association for Supervision and Curriculum Development.

Galdone, P. (1970). *The three little pigs.* New York: Seabury Press.

Gay, M. (2004). *The three little pigs.* Toronto: Groundwood Books.

Gillies, R. M. (2008). The effects of cooperative learning on junior high school students' behaviours, discourse, and learning during a science-based learning activity. *School Psychology International, 29*(3), 328–347.

Gordon, C. (n.d.). *Thinking through the inquiry cycle for young learners*. Accessed at www.slav.vic.edu.au/synergy/volume-10-number-1-2012/research-into-practice/234-thinking-through-the-inquiry-cycle-for-young-learners-.html on August 13, 2016.

Groenke, S. L., & Paulus, T. (2007). The role of teacher questioning in promoting dialogic literary inquiry in computer-mediated communication. *Journal of Research on Technology in Education, 40*(2), 141–164.

Guthrie, J. T. (2001). Contexts for engagement and motivation in reading. *Reading Online, 4*(8).

Hattie, J. (2009). *Visible learning: A synthesis of over 800 meta-analyses relating to achievement*. New York: Routledge.

Hattie, J., & Timperley, H. (2007). The power of feedback. *Review of Educational Research, 77*(1), 81–112.

Ho, A. D., & Kane, T. J. (2013). *The reliability of classroom observations by school personnel* (The MET Project). Seattle, WA: Bill & Melinda Gates Foundation.

Ho, D. G. E. (2005). Why do teachers ask the questions they ask? *RELC Journal, 36*(3), 297–310.

Houck, B., & Novak, S. (2016). *Literacy unleashed: Fostering excellent reading instruction through classroom visits*. Alexandria, VA: Association for Supervision and Curriculum Development.

House, J. D. (2005). Classroom instruction and science achievement in Japan, Hong Kong, and Chinese Taipei: Results from the TIMSS 1999 assessment. *International Journal of Instructional Media, 32*(3), 295–311.

Hulan, N. (2010). What the students will say while the teacher is away: An investigation into student-led and teacher-led discussion within guided reading groups. *Literacy Teaching and Learning, 14*(1–2), 41–64. Accessed at http://files.eric.ed.gov/fulltext/EJ888268.pdf on April 13, 2016.

Hunt, L. M. (2012). *One for the Murphys*. New York: Paulsen Books.

Hunt, L. M. (2015). *Fish in a tree*. New York: Paulsen Books.

International Literacy Association. (n.d.). *Why literacy*? Accessed at www.literacyworldwide.org/why-literacy on April 1, 2016.

Johnson, D. W., & Johnson, F. P. (2006). *Joining together: Group theory and group skills* (9th ed.). Boston: Allyn & Bacon.

Johnson, D. W., & Johnson, R. T. (1985). The internal dynamics of cooperative learning groups. In R. Slavin, S. Sharan, S. Kagan, R. Hertz-Lazarowitz, C. Webb, & R. Schmuck (Eds.), *Learning to cooperate, cooperating to learn* (pp. 103–124). New York: Plenum Press.

Johnson, D. W., & Johnson, R. T. (1990). Cooperative learning and achievement. In S. Sharan (Ed.), *Cooperative learning: Theory and research* (pp. 23–38). New York: Praeger.

Jones, B. (2015). The Confederate flag is a matter of pride and heritage, not hatred [Opinion]. *New York Times*. Accessed at www.nytimes.com/roomfordebate/2015/06/19/does-the-confederate-flag-breed-racism/the-confederate-flag-is-a-matter-of-pride-and-heritage-not-hatred on April 1, 2016.

Kachorek, L. V. (2009). *Using discussion questions effectively*. Ann Arbor, MI: Center for Research on Learning and Teaching. Accessed at www.crlt.umich.edu/node/956 on April 4, 2016.

Kamil, M. L., Borman, G. D., Dole, J., Kral, C. C., Salinger, T., & Torgesen, J. (2008). *Improving adolescent literacy: Effective classroom and intervention practices*. Washington, DC: Institute of Education Sciences.

Law, Y. (2008). Effects of cooperative learning on second graders' learning from text. *Educational Psychology, 28*(5), 567–582.

Lee, H. (1960). *To kill a mockingbird*. Philadelphia: Lippincott.

Lehrer, R., & Schauble, L. (2006). Cultivating model-based reasoning in science education. In R. K. Sawyer (Ed.), *The Cambridge handbook of the learning sciences* (pp. 371–388). Cambridge, MA: Cambridge University Press.

Lingard, B., Hayes, D., & Mills, M. (2003). Teachers and productive pedagogies: Contextualising, conceptualising, utilising. *Pedagogy, Culture, and Society, 11*(3), 399–424.

Loewen, N. (2012). *Believe me, Goldilocks rocks! The story of the three bears as told by Baby Bear*. Mankato, MN: Picture Window Books.

Lord, C. (2015). *A handful of stars*. New York: Scholastic.

Lowell, S. (1992). *The three little javelinas*. Flagstaff, AR: Northland.

Marshall, J. (1988). *Goldilocks and the three bears*. New York: Puffin.

Marshall, J. (1989). *The three little pigs*. New York: Penguin Putnam.

Martin, A. M. (2014). *Rain reign*. New York: Feiwel and Friends.

Martin, L. (n.d.). *Educational benefits of blogging*. Accessed at http://smallbusiness.chron.com/educational-benefits-blogging-27588.html on April 1, 2016.

Marzano, R. J., Pickering, D. J., & Pollock, J. E. (2001). *Classroom instruction that works: Research-based strategies for increasing student achievement*. Alexandria, VA: Association for Supervision and Curriculum Development.

McIntyre, E., Kyle, D. W., & Moore, G. H. (2006). A primary-grade teacher's guidance toward small-group dialogue. *Reading Research Quarterly, 41*(1), 36–66.

Meloth, M. (1991). Enhancing literacy through cooperative learning. In E. H. Hiebert (Ed.), *Literacy for a diverse society: Perspectives, practices, and policies* (pp. 172–183). New York: Teachers College Press.

Mercer, N. (1995). *The guided construction of knowledge: Talk amongst teachers and learners*. Clevedon, England: Multilingual Matters.

Miller, D. (2009). *The book whisperer: Awakening the inner reader in every child*. San Francisco: Jossey-Bass.

Miller, D. (2013). *Reading in the wild: The book whisperer's keys to cultivating lifelong reading habits*. San Francisco: Jossey-Bass.

Mohr, K.J., & Mohr, E.S. (n.d.). *Extending English language learners' classroom interactions using the response protocol*. Reading Rockets website. Accessed at www.readingrockets.org/article/extending-english-language-learners-classroom-interactions-using-response-protocol on August 13, 2016.

Moss, C. M., & Brookhart, S. M. (2012). *Learning targets: Helping students aim for understanding in today's lesson*. Alexandria, VA: Association for Supervision and Curriculum Development.

Murphy, P. K., Wilkinson, I. A. G., Soter, A. O., Hennessey, M. N., & Alexander, J. F. (2009). Examining the effects of classroom discussion on students' comprehension of text: A meta-analysis. *Journal of Educational Psychology, 101*(3), 740–764.

National Council for the Social Studies. (1994). *Expectations of excellence: Curriculum standards for social studies*. Washington, DC: Author.

National Council for the Social Studies. (2013). *College, career, and civic life (C3) framework for social studies state standards: Guidance for enhancing the rigor of K–12 civics, economics, geography, and history*. Silver Spring, MD: Author.

National Council of Teachers of English. (n.d.). *Comprehensive literacy: A policy brief produced by the National Council of Teachers of English*. Accessed at www.ncte.org/library/NCTEFiles/Resources/Journals/CC/0223-mar2013/CC0223PolicyBrief.pdf on August 14, 2016.

National Council of Teachers of Mathematics. (2000). *Principles and standards for school mathematics*. Reston, VA: Author.

National Governors Association Center for Best Practices & Council of Chief State School Officers. (2010a). *Common Core State Standards for English language arts and literacy in history/social studies, science, and technical subjects*. Washington, DC: Authors. Accessed at www.corestandards.org/assets/CCSSI_ELA%20Standards.pdf on April 1, 2016.

National Governors Association Center for Best Practices & Council of Chief State School Officers. (2010b). *Common Core State Standards initiative*. Washington, DC: Authors.

National Governors Association Center for Best Practices & Council of Chief State School Officers. (2010c). *Key shifts in mathematics*. Washington, DC: Authors. Accessed at www.corestandards.org/other-resources/key-shifts-in-mathematics on April 1, 2016.

National Institute of Child Health and Human Development. (2000). *Teaching children to read: An evidence-based assessment of the scientific research literature on reading and its implications for reading instruction* (NIH Publication No. 00–4769). Washington, DC: National Reading Panel.

National Research Council. (1996). *National Science Education Standards: Observe, interact, change, learn*. Washington, DC: National Academy Press.

National Research Council. (2000). *Inquiry and the national science education standards*. Washington, DC: National Academy Press.

Northeast Foundation for Children. (2007). *Responsive classroom: Level I resource book*. Turners Falls, MA: Author.

Novak, S. (2014a). *How to tackle student-led discussions*. Accessed at http://inservice.ascd.org/how-to-tackle-student-led-discussions on August 13, 2016.

Novak, S. (2014b). *Student-led discussions: How do I promote rich conversations about books, videos, and other media?* Alexandria, VA: Association for Supervision and Curriculum Development.

Nystrand, M., Wu, L. L., Gamoran, A., Zeiser, S., & Long, D. A. (2003). Questions in time: Investigating the structure and dynamics of unfolding classroom discourse. *Discourse Processes, 35*(2), 135–198.

Partnership for 21st Century Learning. (n.d.). *Framework for 21st century learning.* Accessed at www.p21.org/our-work/p21-framework on April 1, 2014.

Pearson, P. D., & Gallagher, M. C. (1983). The instruction of reading comprehension. *Contemporary Educational Psychology, 8*(3), 317–344.

Perks, K., & Middleton, M. (2014). Navigating the classroom current. *Educational Leadership, 72*(1), 48–52.

Pichon, L. (2008). *The three horrid little pigs.* Wilton, CT: Tiger Tales.

Polacco, P. (1998). *Thank you, Mr. Falker.* New York: Philomel Books.

Raphael, T. E., & Au, K. H. (2005). QAR: Enhancing comprehension and test taking across grades and content areas. *Reading Teacher, 59*(3), 206– 221.

Robinson, D. H. (1997). Graphic organizers as aids to text learning. *Reading Research and Instruction, 37*(2), 85–105.

Sandwell, R. (2005). School history versus the historians. *International Journal of Social Education, 20*(1), 9–15.

Sartain, L., Stoelinga, S. R., & Brown, E. R. (2011). *Rethinking teacher evaluation in Chicago: Lessons learned from classroom observations, principal-teacher conferences, and district implementation* [Research report]. Chicago: Consortium on Chicago School Research, University of Chicago.

Schunk, D. H. (1998). Goal and self-evaluative influences during children's cognitive skill learning. *American Educational Research Journal, 33*(2), 359–382.

Schwartz, C. R. (2012). *The three ninja pigs.* New York: Putnam's.

Scieszka, J. (1989). *The true story of the three little pigs.* New York: Viking Books.

Dr. Seuss (1971). *The Lorax.* New York: Random House.

Shaw, D. (2005). *Retelling strategies to improve comprehension: Effective hands-on strategies for fiction and nonfiction that help students remember and understand what they read.* New York: Scholastic.

Slavin, R. E. (1987). Cooperative learning and the cooperative school. *Educational Leadership, 45*(3), 7–13.

Slavin, R. E. (1995). *Cooperative learning: Theory, research, and practice* (2nd ed.). Boston: Allyn & Bacon.

Snider, A. (n.d.). *Debate as a method for improving critical thinking and creativity.* World Debate Institute, University of Vermont. Accessed at http://debate.uvm.edu/travel/china/chinaspeng.html on August 14, 2016.

Stigler, J. W., & Hiebert, J. (1999). *The teaching gap: Best ideas from the world's teachers for improving education in the classroom.* New York: Free Press.

Stover, K., & Yearta, L. (2017). *From pencils to podcasts: Digital tools for transforming K–6 literacy practices.* Bloomington: Solution Tree Press.

Surowiecki, J. (2004). *The wisdom of crowds: Why the many are smarter than the few and how collective wisdom shapes business, economies, societies, and nations.* New York: Doubleday.

Tatum, A. W. (2013). *Fearless voices: Engaging a new generation of African American adolescent male writers.* New York: Scholastic Teaching Resources.

Teague, M. (2013). *The three little pigs and the somewhat bad wolf.* New York: Orchard Books.

Thome, C. (n.d.). *Bringing the Common Core standards to life in the classroom.* Accessed at www.readinga-z.com/research/bringing-the-common-core-standards-to-life-in-the-classroom.pdf on April 1, 2016.

Torgesen, J. K., Houston, D. D., Rissman, L. M., Decker, S. M., Roberts, G., Vaughn, S., Wexler, J. Francis, D. J, Rivera, M. O., Lesaux, N. (2007). *Academic literacy instruction for adolescents: A guidance document from the Center on Instruction.* Portsmouth, NH: RMC Research Corporation, Center on Instruction.

Trivizas, E. (1993). *The three little wolves and the big bad pig.* New York: McElderry Books.

Vogler, K. E. (2008). Asking good questions. *Educational Leadership, 65*(9). Accessed at www.ascd.org/publications/educational-leadership/summer08/vol65/num09/Asking-Good-Questions.aspx on April 1, 2016.

Wagner, T. (2010). *The global achievement gap: Why even our best schools don't teach the new survival skills our children need—And what we can do about it.* New York: Basic Books.

Wagner, T. (2012). *Creating innovators: The making of young people who will change the world.* New York: Scribner.

Walsh, J. A., & Sattes, B. D. (2015). *Questioning for classroom discussion: Purposeful speaking, engaged listening, deep thinking.* Alexandria, VA: Association for Supervision and Curriculum Development.

Wiesner, D. (2001). *The three pigs.* New York: Clarion Books.

Wilhelm, J. D., & Smith, M. W. (2014). *Reading unbound: Why kids need to read what they want—And why we should let them.* New York: Scholastic.

Woodson, J. (2001). *The other side.* New York: Putnam's.

York-Barr, J., Sommers, W. A., Ghere, G. S., & Montie, J. K. (2006). *Reflective practice to improve schools: An action guide for educators* (2nd ed.). Thousand Oaks, CA: Corwin Press.

Zemelman, S., Daniels, H., & Hyde, A. (1993). *Best practice: New standards for teaching and learning in America's schools.* Portsmouth, NH: Heinemann.

# Index

## T



## W



## Y

**Motivating Students**
***Carolyn Chapman and Nicole Dimich Vagle***
Learn why students disengage and how to motivate them to achieve success with a five-step framework. Research-based strategies and fun activities, along with tips and troubleshooting advice, show how to instill a lasting love of learning in students of any age.
**BKF371**

**Instructional Methods for Differentiation & Deeper Learning**
***James H. Stronge and Xianxuan Xu***
Discover research-based strategies for differentiated instruction that teachers, coaches, and administrators can use to enhance their everyday practices. Explore ways to implement differentiated learning for both students needing personalized remedial instruction and high-ability students, as well as tactics for executing instruction in culturally diverse classrooms.
**BKF700**

**The Five Dimensions of Engaged Teaching**
***Laura Weaver and Mark Wilding***
*Engaged teaching* recognizes that educators need to offer more than lesson plans and assessments for students to thrive in the 21st century. Equip your students to be resilient individuals, able to communicate effectively and work with diverse people.
**BKF601**

**Unstoppable Learning**
***Douglas Fisher and Nancy Frey***
Discover proven methods to enhance teaching and learning schoolwide. Identify questions educators should ask to guarantee a positive classroom culture where students learn from each other, not just teachers. Explore ways to adapt teaching in response to students' individual needs.
**BKF662**

**Transformative Teaching**
***Kathleen Kryza, MaryAnn Brittingham, and Alicia Duncan***
Examine the most effective strategies for leading diverse students to develop the skills they need inside and outside the classroom. By understanding and exploring students' emotional, cultural, and academic needs, educators will be better prepared to help *all* students become lifelong learners.
**BKF623**

Solution Tree | Press 

Visit SolutionTree.com or call 800.733.6786 to order.